THE BLACK CAT

THE BLACK CAT

Edited By
Philip J. Riley

Production History
By
Gregory Wm. Mank

The Black Cat: Universal's Symphony of Horrors
The Film's Music
by Randall D. Larson

UNIVERSAL SERIES
VOLUME 18
MagicImage Filmbooks is an imprint of
BearManor Media

BearManor Media

www.bearmanormedia.com

Library of Congress Control Number: 2015909446
ISBN: 1-59393-779-2

Editor-in-Chief - Philip J. Riley

The Black Cat is available from Universal Home Entertainment and as part of the "Bela Lugosi Collection."

The Black Cat: Universal's Symphony of Horrors - The Film's Music - by Randall D. Larson ©2015

Production History by Gregory Wm. Mank ©2015

Special art-work by Al Magliochetti

Table of Contents

"THE BLACK CAT" — A Universal Production PRINTED IN U. S. A.

Prologue

May God shield and deliver me from the fangs of the Arch-Fiend!

From Edgar Allan Poe's tale, *The Black Cat* (1843)

An aerial View of Golden Age Universal

4:00 p.m., March 14, 1934.

The sun shines over the purple mountain at Universal City, California, out in the wilds of the San Fernando Valley. As sheep graze on the hillside, a crazy pastorale takes place below. It's a "Black Cats Parade," celebrated to select a feline for the title role in the "KARLOFF and BELA LUGOSI" vehicle, *The Black Cat.*

A festive crowd, largely made up of star-struck young ladies, giggling children, and their jittery cats, files past the newsreel camera. As *Variety* will headline the next morning:

300 Cats and Temperament

There's KARLOFF, as Universal exalts him (by surname only), *The Black* Cat's sly, silver fox of an Anti-Christ—gaunt, adorned in a long, black robe, his satanic hairdo cut into a "V," his dark brown eyes twinkling, smiling at all beholders through his black lipstick.

He's the star who made Frankenstein's Monster both horrifying and heartbreaking.

Then there's BELA LUGOSI, (billed by first and last names), *The Black Cat's* diabolical avenging angel — dashingly handsome, wearing a matinee idol dressing gown, his blue eyes crinkling, appearing to be genuinely enjoying himself, despite his Old Country aversion to cats.

He's the man who made Dracula both sinister and seductive.

A little girl named Bernice, who brought her cat "Jiggs," campaigns for victory by performing acrobatics, walking on her hands. Karloff and Lugosi proclaim her and Jiggs the winners. Bernice gets $25, while Jiggs lands a cameo in the movie - or so Universal promises.

The "Black Cats Parade" is, as *Variety* calls it, "a howling success."

Yet something perverse is at play here. A starlet from *The Black Cat*, naughtily nicknamed "The Virgin Mary" at Universal, shyly watches the parade, in her flowing blonde hair and slinky black negligee, a victim of sexual harassment she shamefully keeps a secret. Inside a soundstage looms the film's tall, cockeyed Black Mass cross, in blasphemous defiance of the censors. And there's a horrific rack, upon which Karloff's Devil hangs and yelps in the film as Lugosi skins him - a virtual crucifixion of Satan. The original script calls for Karloff's skinned-alive Lucifer to wriggle off the rack, splatting, crawling, a hideous bloody pulp, lasciviously eking his way across the floor toward the auburn-haired heroine, Lugosi laughing at him, "hysterically, insanely..."

Meanwhile, on this day, as if sensing the dark nature of this most audacious of Universal's horror classics, the cats go wild. Several run away from their masters and mistresses, forming a coven under the bungalow of Warren Doane, head of Universal's short subjects branch. There they stay, as *Variety* reports, "hissing off all attempts at rescue."

As Edgar Allan Poe wrote in his *Instinct vs. Reason*, "for it will be remembered that black cats are all of them witches."

The Black Cat was a real-life melodrama, and its twists were many: Father vs. son enmity, inspiration from a haunted World War I fortress where 679 German soldiers burned to death, a homage to the self-proclaimed "Beast of the Apocalypse" and his "Scarlet Woman," Pre-Code censorship battles, an outrageously skimpy budget and shooting schedule, a shocking sexual harassment on-set saga, wacky publicity, an emergency day-and-night retake session, exile for its director, a vicious critical onslaught, an amazingly responsive box office...and the first bewitching union of KARLOFF and BELA LUGOSI, and what became their complex, tragic relationship.

This volume, with full production history, and the pressbook, tells the complete story.

Karloff and Lugosi with winners Bernice Firestine, Evelyn Eady, and Bobbie Hayner - Courtesy of Bernice Firestine McGee.

CHAPTER 1

"UNCLE CARL" AND HIS 67-POUND BIRTHDAY CAKE

Universal was an eccentric studio and "Uncle Carl" was an eccentric, dear, crazy old man – let's face it!
Shirley Ulmer, assistant script clerk on *The Black Cat*, widow of Edgar G. Ulmer, and former Laemmle-in-law.

January 17, 1934: Carl Laemmle, Sr.'s 67th birthday. From left to right: Boris Karloff, Hugh Enfield (aka Craig Reynolds), Ken Maynard, "Uncle Carl", Vince Barnett, Margaret Sullavan, Andy Devine, and Carl Laemmle, Jr.

Wednesday, January 17, 1934: It's Carl Laemmle, Sr.'s 67th birthday, and his giant chocolate cake weighs precisely 67 pounds.

Universal gathers at noon to celebrate. Among those posing for pictures at the party with the grand old man are his 25-year old son, Carl Laemmle, Jr., Universal's "Crown Prince"; Margaret Sullavan, who's just starred in Universal's tear jerker *Only Yesterday*; and on the right hand of the founder, Boris Karloff.

"It was always a happy lot," Karloff would say of Universal late-in-life.

Yet note Karloff's wry grin in the photo, as if he's

wishing he could escape this ritual and go play at the Hollywood Cricket Club. He's risen at Universal as a world-famous star: the hapless Monster of *Frankenstein*, the rampaging butler of *The Old Dark House*, the lovelorn Im-Ho-Tep of *The Mummy*. The studio has been almost delirious in it star campaign: indeed, the posters for *The Mummy* proclaimed him as "KARLOFF the Uncanny."

Yet the Uncanny one has had his share of sufferings on "the happy lot":

• There was *Frankenstein*, where director James Whale sadistically ordered Karloff to run up a back lot hill to the windmill with Colin Clive over his shoulder, under a full moon, the torch-bearing villagers in pur-

11

suit, over and over again. The atrocity seemed Calvary-inspired – Whale as Pilate, Karloff the Christ, Clive the cross — and left Karloff with life-long back trouble.

• There was *The Mummy*, with Karloff enduring eight hours of caking and wrapping in Jack P. Pierce's brilliant makeup, the costume leaving no place for his body to breathe. Deprived of oxygen, Karloff passed out, falling out of the casket and right on his face. To add to his suffering, the costume had no fly.

• There was *The Ghoul*, Karloff's first visit to his homeland England since 1909. He wanted to stay for a while, but Universal demanded he return to play *The Invisible Man*. He did, only to learn the studio was negotiating with William Powell to play the Invisible One. Meanwhile, Universal had refused to raise Karloff's salary as promised.

Claude Rains eventually starred as the Invisible Man, and Karloff had walked out of Universal.

Now he's back - a founder of the Screen Actors Guild (membership card no. 9), having completed juicy roles in RKO's *The Lost Patrol* and 20th Century's *House of Rothschild*, earning a new, improved Universal salary,

and set to reprise his "dear old Monster" in a sequel tentatively titled *The Return of Frankenstein*. Yet a new horror film will precede the Monster's misadventures. On the same day that Universal celebrates Laemmle, Sr.'s birthday, *Variety* reports page one news: Universal will produce a new Universal horror show, *The Black Cat*, "based on the Edgar Allen (sic) Poe story" and as "a starrer for Karloff. "

Laemmle, Jr. hopes to make this film his most grisly shocker to date. There's a reason for it.

In the birthday pictures, "Junior" Laemmle's Mr. Sardonicus smile hides a very unhappy man. *Dracula*, produced by Junior, had reaped a world-wide rental of $1.2 million; *Frankenstein*, his horror follow-up, $1.4 million. The horror classics crowned Universal with a corporate identity it still enjoys over 80 years later. But Laemmle, Sr. thinks Laemmle, Jr.'s horrors "morbid." *Dracula*, a sex fiend from Hell who drinks the blood of virgins. *Frankenstein*, a scientist who defies God by creating a Monster, stitched together from corpses.

"Why don't we make *dog* pictures?" bitches the old man.

Junior was General Manager of Universal City even

before his 21st birthday on April 28, 1929. Battles began immediately. There was *All Quiet on the Western Front*, which had premiered in Los Angeles April 21, 1930, a week before Junior's 22nd birthday. Laemmle, Sr. had vehemently protested filming Erich Maria Remarque's novel, yet Laemmle, Jr. had proceeded. The international smash hit earned rentals of $3,000,000 and won the Academy Award for Best Picture of 1930.

Carl Laemmle Sr., accepting the Best Picture Academy Award for All Quiet on the Western Front *at a Universal ceremony, shortly after the actual Academy Awards dinner. Conrad Nagel presents the award to Uncle Carl, while Universal contractee Slim Summerville, who appeared in the film, observes. Significantly, Junior Laemmle is not in the picture.*

Proudly accepting the award, despite his tantrums about the epic: Carl Laemmle, Sr.

It's largely a battle of vision: Junior dares to expand the Universal product, so to vie with the best of MGM, Paramount and Warner Bros. "Uncle Carl" wants things cheap and simple. Publicly, the patriarch hails his son, but privately they fight bitterly.

Yet the bitterest fight has been a personal one. Junior had wanted to marry Constance Cummings, a blonde, very talented actress. However, Constance wasn't Jewish, and Laemmle, Sr. vowed he'd destroy Junior and disinherit him if he wed the "shiksa." On July 3, 1933, Constance married Benn Levy, who'd scripted *The Old Dark House*. She then continued an acting career that would last for over half-a-century.

Junior reportedly never recovered.

Carl Laemmle, Sr. was a beloved man – a Hollywood pioneer who performed many heroically kind acts for his family and friends. Yet he was his own son's worst nightmare. At this time, Shirley Kassler was a Laemmle-in-law, married to Uncle Carl's favorite nephew Max Alexander, himself a film producer. She recalled in an interview with this author in 1988:

It was amazing! At the big Laemmle estate in Benedict Canyon, every Sunday, we all came into the dining room, maybe 24 strong – all relatives. We were not allowed to speak or sit until Uncle Carl had made his entrance. Since he was always fighting with his son, poor Junior, and his daughter Rosabelle, I finally got the seat of honor at the table, next to Uncle Carl...

So...Junior seeks revenge on his despotic father: He'll produce his most shocking horror film to date. He believes he knows just the man to deliver it. Not James Whale, who directed *Frankenstein*, *The Old Dark House*, and *The Invisible Man*; not Karl Freund, who'd directed *The Mummy*. The director-to-be is attending the birthday party, way in the back row of celebrants. He's 29-years old, has a mane of wavy black hair, and a mustache that unfortunately resembles that worn by the man who, in August that year, will become the Fuhrer of Germany.

As *Variety* had headlined that morning of January 17, "Edgar Ulmer To Meg 'Black Cat'".

Constance Cummings, whom Junior Laemmle wanted to marry. Laemmle Sr. forbade it.

13

CHAPTER 2

ENTER THE OOFLYDORF

My father was a gremlin! He could go between being very scary and being very funny. He loved to scare people – it's a Germanic thing – and if I was bad as a little girl, he'd tell me the "ooflydoof" (he invented language!) was going to come out of the closet and get me! It really scared me, but it's a very funny word, right?

Arianne Ulmer, daughter of Edgar G. Ulmer.

Portrait of Edgar G. Ulmer, circa 1924

Born September 17, 1904 in Olmutz, Moravia, in the Czech Republic, and raised in Vienna, Edgar George Ulmer was a Teutonic boy wonder with the soubriquet "The Aesthete from the Alps" and an astoundingly rich resume – or so he claimed. Was he really a set designer (at age 15) on Paul Wegener's *The Golem* (1920)? Was he actually the art director on Erich Von Stroheim's *Merry-Go-Round* (1923)? Was he truly the assistant art director on Cecil B. DeMille's *The King of Kings* (1927)? Did he in fact direct the German version of Garbo's *Anna Christie* (1930)?

In his acclaimed 2014 biography, *Edgar G. Ulmer: A Filmmaker at the Margins*, Noah Isenberg separates the myth from the reality, admitting that the mists of time have made impossible proving (or disproving) many of Ulmer's claims. Nevertheless, Isenberg's research nails down some facts:

• Ulmer was a student of the legendary director/set designer Max Reinhardt.
• Ulmer had been at Universal from 1924 to 1928,

working as an assistant set designer for Charles D. Hall and directing two-reel westerns.

- Away from Universal, Ulmer had collaborated with set designer Rochus Gliese on Fox's *Sunrise* (1927), directed by F.W. Murnau. The film features the all-in-black "Woman from the City" (Margaret Livingston), who only comes out at night, seduces "The Man" (George O'Brien) in a swamp under a full moon, demanding he drown "The Wife" (Janet Gaynor). *Sunrise* won a "Best Picture, Unique and Artistic Production" Academy Award and Gliese was Academy-nominated for the set design.

- In Germany, Ulmer had co-directed (with Robert Siodmak) the acclaimed *People on Sunday* (1930).

- Back in Hollywood, Ulmer had directed Columbia's *Damaged Lives* (1933), a saga about a married couple who suffer the horrors of syphilis.

The man has flair, brilliance, and a sense of the demonic. It's about this time that Shirley Kassler crosses his path. As she told me in 1988:

I fell in love with Edgar the first time I met him – the first time I heard him. I was in the kitchen in my Hollywood apartment (trying to make a pot roast!). He had come in with some friends. I heard this thunderous voice – and I started to shiver. I thought, "I want to meet this man!" There he was, with the moustache and the wild hair – he was everything I would never have thought I'd care for – but I thought he needed me.

She'd driven with Edgar to the beach that night, falling in love by the Pacific. For the time being, she stays married to Max. "Uncle Carl," meanwhile, knows nothing of the situation.

Edgar is a close friend of Junior's, who, as Shirley remembered, was "psycho." Yet in Junior's mind, Edgar is the madman, with unbridled imagination and a deep darkness. If Junior wants a new horror film that will scare the hell out of his father, Edgar G. Ulmer is his man to deliver it, and Junior gives him autonomy to direct, as well as fashion the story, sets and costumes. As Ulmer himself will tell Peter Bogdanovich late-in-life in an interview published in the anthology, *Kings of the Bs*:

...Junior gave me free rein to write a horror picture in the style we had started in Europe with Caligari (1920). And he gave me my head for the first time. He was a very, very strange producer; he didn't have much education, but he had great respect for intelligence and creative spirit.

And so, as Carl Laemmle, Sr.'s 67th birthday party goes rollicking along, and Junior, Boris and Edgar join the gang in singing "Happy Birthday," "Uncle Carl" is mercifully unaware of what this trio will soon be doing to give him nightmares. Yet it's all destined to become even more ghastly.

Two days later, January 19, *The Hollywood Reporter* announces that Universal is seeking Bela Lugosi to join *The Black Cat*.

CHAPTER 3

BELA'S NIGHTMARE

I created my own Frankenstein Monster!
Bela Lugosi, regarding Boris Karloff's casting as the Monster in *Frankenstein*.

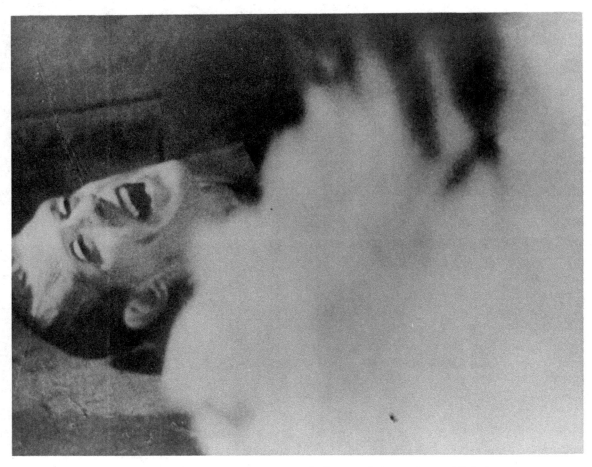

The image of Karloff's Monster burning in the windmill in Frankenstein *haunted Bela Lugosi.*

After *Frankenstein* had opened sensationally New Year's Day of 1932 at Los Angeles' Orpheum Theatre, Bela Lugosi curiously went to see it. He afterwards confessed to Hungarian friends that the film had genuinely disturbed him. The image of Karloff's Monster, crying and screaming as he burned alive in the windmill, deeply upset Lugosi, he claimed, because the creature reminded him of soldiers Bela had seen dying in anguish in World War I. He'd heard the wounded men crying for their mothers; he'd smelled the burning flesh.

His Hungarian friends remembered Bela imitating the Monster, waving his hands as if to keep away the flames. Bela Lugosi was an emotional man, and even just recalling the scene, it moved him to tears.

Of course, after his brilliant success as Universal's

Dracula, Bela had tested as the Monster in *Frankenstein* during the haunted summer of 1931, Universal's first choice for the role. He'd declared the role unworthy.

"I was a star in my country, and will not be a scarecrow over here!" Bela said.

He'd claimed (and would repeat the claim many times in the future) that he'd "discovered" Boris Karloff, suggesting him for *Frankenstein*. Although evidence suggests the final decision actually came from James Whale, who preferred Karloff, and that Junior Laemmle, pampering Whale, agreed, the full truth is perhaps lost to the ages. At any rate, Lugosi quickly saw the calamity after *Frankenstein's* sensational popularity.

Lugosi has scored post-*Frankenstein* 1932 hits: mad

"DRACULA" A Universal Production MADE IN U.S.A.

Bela Lugosi as Dracula (1931)

Dr. Mirakle in Universal's *Murders in the Rue Morgue*; Murder Legendre in United Artists' *White Zombie*; Roxor in Fox's *Chandu the Magician*. But in October of 1932, his lavish generosity and bad business sense have plunged him into bankruptcy, and the movie colony has not responded with kindness. Paramount, aware of his financial woes, quickly engaged Bela to play the hirsute "Sayer of the Law" in *Island of Lost Souls*, starring Charles Laughton as whip-cracking Dr. Moreau and Kathleen Burke, winner of Paramount's national "Panther Woman" contest. Laughton signs for $10,125; Burke, in her film debut, for $1,000.

Lugosi in Broadway's "Murder at the Vanities" (1933)

Lugosi does excerpts from Dracula *and then, apparently by design, breaks down such effect as he may have created with a comedy curtain speech which he opens with the hope that audiences will not suffer from the chills...Lugosi would leave a stronger impression sticking to character.*

One can't blame Bela if he never wants to work in Hollywood again, or at least at Universal – which, despite the fortune *Dracula* earned for the studio, made no offers to him during his publicized money troubles.

Monday, January 22, 1934: "Lugosi Buys Play," headlines *The Hollywood Reporter:*

New York – Bela Lugosi has acquired a play with Spring production planned by Chicago. It is Pagan Fury, by S. J. Warshawsky, and Lugosi will star.

Friday, January 26: The Laemmles Sr. and Jr. leave on *The Chief* this night for a business trip to New York City. Meanwhile, Lugosi, in New York, must decide if he wishes to devote his huge dramatic energy to *Pagan Fury*, in which he'll portray a Bohemian artist, or head west to the arena where he "created his own Monster." It's a Monster that not only reminds him of the horrors of World War I, but also of what might be the most damaging career twist of his life.

If he decides the latter, it will mean co-starring with the "Monster" as well.

Bela's contracted salary for *Island of Lost Souls*: $875 for the entire picture.

Yet the man is seemingly indomitable. On January 31, 1933, he marries 21-year old Lillian Arch. He takes what film offers he can get, including a wonderful comic heavy in Paramount's *International House*, in which he snarls at W.C. Fields. In the summer of 1933, he becomes an early member of the Screen Actors Guild (membership card no. 28). With Hollywood cold, he takes off for Broadway, opening in September in Earl Carroll's racy *Murder at the Vanities*, co-starring with *Freaks'* Olga Baclanova and a bevy of chorines Carroll boasts as being "the most beautiful girls in the world." He leaves the musical in December, cleared of bankruptcy.

January, 1934: Bela Lugosi is still in New York City. His current gig is vaudeville - an 18-minute version of *Dracula. Variety* catches the act in December at Broadway's State Theatre, where the stage show supports the Paul Muni Warner Bros. feature *The World Changes*, and where Bela shares the bill with an acrobatic act, a comic, a singer, various stooges, a toe dancer who performs a "semi-strip" (that is, according to *Variety*, "too brief for the men in the audience"), and a show-stealing 12-piece girl band. As for Bela's act, *Variety* writes:

Lugosi with his wife Lillian,
shortly after their 1933 wedding

CHAPTER 4
"FORT DOUAMONT", "THE BEAST" AND THE "SCARLET WOMAN"

I rave, I rape, I rip, I rend....
From Aleister Crowley's *A Hymn to Pan.*

(above - Fort Douamont
(Left) Edgar Allan Poe

Universal already has three scripts by the title of *The Black Cat.* One of them actually bears a resemblance to Poe's work.

The Black Cat, originally published August 19, 1843 in *The Saturday Evening Post*, is one of Poe's most sadistic stories – basically an exorcism of the author's own tragic alcoholism. The narrator, a raging drunk, comes home one night from a tavern and assaults his pet black cat, "Pluto." The atrocity: gouging out one of the cat's eyes with a pen knife. Later, he takes the cat out in the garden, hangs it, and kills it. But that night, mysteriously, the house catches afire – and when the narrator returns, he finds on the surviving wall the shadow of a cat, complete with a rope around his neck.

The narrator adopts a new black cat; strangely, it even has only one eye. Soon he notices a white spot on the cat's chest, that grows to resemble...a gallows. Eventually the narrator tries to kill the cat with an axe and, unfortunately for his wife, she tries to save the cat.

Goaded, by the interference, into a rage more than demoniacal, I withdrew my arm from her grasp and buried the axe in her brain. She fell dead upon the spot, without a groan.

He walls up the body in the cellar. The cat seemingly disappears. Police come to investigate the wife's disappearance. A wail rises up from behind the cellar wall:

a howl – a wailing shriek, half of horror and half of triumph, such as might have arisen only out of hell, conjointly from the throats of the damned in their agony and of the demons that exult in the damnation...

The police tear down the wall, and see the wife's carcass ("already greatly decayed and clotted with gore"), the one-eyed black cat sitting on her head.

"I had walled the monster up within the tomb!" reads the final sentence.

Richard Schayer, Universal's scenario editor, had written a 1932 script for *The Black Cat*, following the basic story with Karloff set as the sadistic drunk, toyingly named "Edgar Doe." Two more drafts followed by other writers with wildly different storylines (see the end notes).

Edgar Ulmer has a new approach.

Out goes Poe's original tale, along with the previous screenplays. Ulmer remembers Gustav Meyrink, (1868-1932), who'd written *Der Golem* as a 1915 novel. Ulmer would describe Meyrink as a man "like Kafka, who was very much tied up in the mystic Talmudic background." He recalled Meyrink was envisioning a play on a French fortress shelled by the Germans during World War I. The name was of the fortress was Fort Douamont.

Douamont, the largest, highest fortress of 19 protecting Verdun, fell to the Kaiser February 25, 1916. However, it achieved its grisly infamy on May 8, 1916, when German soldiers, carelessly warming their coffee with fuel from flamethrowers (!), accidentally detonated shells, setting off an inferno that roared through the fort, burning alive 679 men. Similar to the unfortunate wife in Poe's *The Black Cat*, the soldiers received burial in the fort's cellar and behind a wall; the site is a German war grave. The French forces recaptured Douamont October 24, 1916.

"...the commander was a strange Euripides figure," said Ulmer, "who went crazy three years later when he was brought back to Paris, because he had walked on that mountain of bodies."

Meanwhile, Ulmer has a collaborator: George Carol Sims, who has two *noms de plume*. As Paul Cain, he pens "hard-boiled detective novelettes" for *Black Mask* magazine; as Peter Ruric, he writes screenplays. Described by film historian Dennis Fischer as "a blond, bearded member of the Malibu Beach crowd, taken to wearing ascot scarves," Ruric is the lover of actress Gertrude Michael, who in 1934, wins her own Pre-Code Hollywood infamy, singing "Sweet Marijuana" in Paramount's *Murder at the Vanities*.

Germany had made a film, *Douamont: The Hell of Verdun* (1931), with German officers serving as technical advisors. For *The Black Cat*, Ulmer changes the name to "Fort Marmaros," which is an inside joke: the "Marmorhaus" is a theatre in Berlin, translated as "Marblehouse," its façade in fact covered in marble. It's a sacred site for Ulmer: the Marmorhaus had hosted the February 26, 1920 premiere of *The Cabinet of Dr. Caligari*.

Yet Ulmer wants more than the "Hell" of Douamont/Marmaros. He wants to power-pack *The Black Cat* with the fire-and-brimstone Hell, the Hell of Lucifer.

Strangely enough, he finds a real-life inspiration.

"The Wickedest Man in the World" is the soubriquet enjoyed by Aleister Crowley, a Satanist who, with a shaved head and sharpened teeth, proudly proclaims himself "The Beast of the Apocalypse."

Born in Leamington, England on October 12, 1875, the son of hysterically religious parents, Crowley had been a wealthy heir, mountain climber, writer, poet, chess player, sex maniac, drug addict, and high priest, professing a satanic theology: "Do what thou wilt/shall be the whole of the Law." He'd peaked in 1920, when he founded the Abbey of Thelema in a farmhouse in Cefalu, Sicily, on the Tyrrhenian Sea. There, Crowley celebrated satanic rites with his "Scarlet Woman" mistress, Leah Hirsig, who had her own macabre credo:

I will work for wickedness. I will kill my heart, I will be shameless before all men, I will freely prostitute my body to all creatures.

In his excellent book *Do What Thou Wilt: A Life of Aleister Crowley*, Lawrence Sutin writes of the Abbey of Thelema, its six-sided altar, its view of the sea, and:

The bedroom that Crowley shared with Hirsig...he named "Le Chambre des Cauchemars" – The Room of Nightmares. It was on the walls of this room that Crowley the artist created his masterpiece – an astonishing montage (as revealed by photographs taken in the 1950s by Kenneth Anger) of unbridled sexuality, blasphemy, poetry, and magical prophecy...On the main wall of the Chambre was a tableau entitled "HELL-La Nature Malade," which included, as a centerpiece, a leering portrait of a red-lipped Hirsig and a quotation from the poem "Leah Sublime, " an homage to the Scarlet Woman composed by Crowley in June 1920: "Stab your demoniac smile to my brain,/Soak me in cognac, cunt, and cocaine."

One witness reported a Black Mass in which the "Scarlet Woman" engaged in bestiality with a goat, after which the goat's throat was slashed and blood poured over the naked back of another woman. On February 16, 1923, an Oxford undergraduate named Raoul Loveday died, possibly after drinking the blood of a sacrificial cat at Crowley's temple, although a more likely reason of death was bad water from a mountain spring. There was a wild public scandal, and Benito Mussolini exiled Crowley from Sicily.

In 1932, artist Nina Hamnett, the model for Henry Gaudier-Brzeska's sculpture "Laughing Torso," wrote in her memoir (also titled *Laughing Torso*) that's she'd been an acquaintance of "the Beast," that he was supposed to have practiced Black Magic at his abbey in Cefalu, that a baby was said to have mysteriously disappeared, that Crowley had a goat, and that the villagers "were frightened of him." Crowley, who'd squandered most of his inheritance by this time, decided to sue.

"The Beast" was preparing his lawsuit as Universal was concocting *The Black Cat*.

The raving, raping, ripping and rending of Aleister Crowley fascinated Edgar Ulmer; critically, they became the influence that truly made *The Black Cat* a horror film. The role Ulmer fashioned for "KARLOFF the Uncanny" was remarkable. Remembering Fritz Lang (whom Ulmer had described as "a sadist of the worst order you can imagine"), lifting the "Poelzig" from Dr. Hans Poelzig (masterful architect and designer of 1920's *Der Golem*), borrowing the "Hjalmar" from *The Wild Duck* by Ibsen (whom Ulmer admired deeply), and taking inspiration from Crowley's "Beast," Ulmer created Hjalmar Poelzig, High Priest of a Lucifer cult in the Carpathian mountains. Here was a betrayer, murderer, and necrophile, who sacrifices virgins, kills his wife, weds his stepdaughter, poses female corpses in glass coffins in his cellar, and dies skinned alive on his own "embalming rack." It was as vile a villain as the cinema, horror genre or otherwise, had ever beheld.

Would the pet-and-poetry Karloff accept so vile a role?

Aleister Crowley. "the Beast of the Apocalypse".

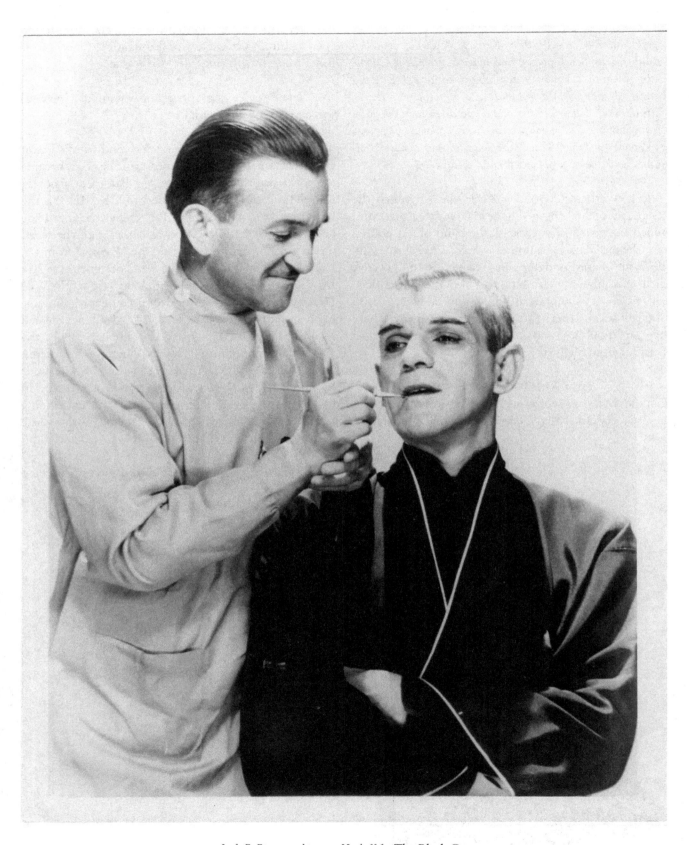

Jack P. Pierce making up Karloff for The Black Cat

CHAPTER 5

"Dear Boris," Edgar the Swan, and Bela Makes a Choice

...it dates right back to Mother Eve, who perhaps revealed that Evil is much more fascinating than Good when she allowed the serpent to merchandize his apple.

Boris Karloff, "Hollywood's Forbidden Face," *Screen Play* Magazine, 1934.

The Boris Karloff house, 9936 Toluca Lake Avenue, where he lived at the time of The Black Cat.

Karloff at Toluca Lake with his wife Dorothy and the swans.

Boris Karloff and his wife Dorothy live in a Spanish bungalow on the shore of Toluca Lake in North Hollywood. Boris strolls along the lake, privately relaxing in top hat and elastic swim trunks called "wickies," playing with his dogs and feeding the swans. Indeed, with his St. Francis of Assisi-style love of animals, Boris has won distinction at Toluca Lake – he's made friends with a large, hissing swan who's been terrorizing the area. In fact, Karloff has named the swan "Edgar" (after the Edgar Swann store in London). His taming of the swan is amazing, especially since Edgar had recently attacked Boris's neighbor W.C. Fields, knocking Fields out of his canoe, beating him with his wings, and trying to drown him!

Little wonder Hollywood-at-large regards him as "Dear Boris."

Karloff has the clout to bail out of the new Universal project and demand a different role if *The Black Cat* offends him. However, he's delighted. As the star tells *Screen Play* magazine:

There's a little bit of evil in us all... Most people – even most actors – don't get the chance that is mine to indulge this inherently bad streak...I insist on taking on not only the exterior

appearance of the creature but also his psychology as completely as possible for me to do. This allows me an escape from myself... When I am through with a character, he has definitely vanished and with him all that is unsettled and restless in my being. I have done with the fellow, so to speak, and you have no idea what a contented state results!

Karloff finds Ulmer's aura and cinematic approach strangely appealing. Ulmer will tell *Modern Monsters* magazine in 1966:

...On The Black Cat, *I designed the sets, that "way-out" house, and, if you really want to know, Mr. Karloff's wardrobe...One of the things he found most exciting in this film was the wardrobe...He felt in these duds, he could employ a sort of "out-of-this-world" appearance. That, as you know, was exactly as he appeared.*

Jack Pierce, working along with Ulmer's conceptions, will make a kinky devil out of Boris for *The Black Cat*, providing a triangular coiffure, white greasepaint, black lipstick, and teased (as well as teasing) eyebrows worthy of a depraved 1920s Berlin chorus girl. Karloff will appear as a fey but fierce Fallen Angel...or perhaps, in his sashed black robe, a transvestite witch.

Monday, February 12: Three significant events occur related to *The Black Cat*.

Boris Karloff makes a personal appearance at the Golden Gate Theatre in San Francisco, where *The Lost Patrol* is a smash hit. Karloff's role is Sanders, a wild-eyed religious lunatic in this taut, John Ford-directed saga of British soldiers, dying one-by-one as Arab snipers strike in the Mesopotamia Desert. Boris cries, creeps, cackles, and for a topper, walks into the dunes and the Arab gunfire, wearing sackcloth and carrying a makeshift cross, like Jesus marching to his crucifixion.

Also February 12: David Manners, romantic lead of *Dracula*, *The Mummy*, and *The Death Kiss*, comes back to Hollywood tonight from New York, where he'd returned after a trip to England to film *The Luck of a Sailor*.

However, the most significant news is that, on this date, Bela Lugosi — who on Saturday night, February 10, had been guest of honor at the Hungarian Actors Ball at the Pennsylvania Hotel in New York City — makes a decision. As *The Hollywood Reporter* will write the next morning:

Lugosi Returns for "U's" "Black Cat"

Bela Lugosi yesterday decided to give up his personal appearances in the east and accept Universal's offer for a featured spot in The Black Cat, *which Edgar Ullmer (sic) directs with Boris Karloff in the lead. Peter Ruric is scripting the Edgar Allan Poe story. Lugosi arrives here February 21. Al Kingston set the deal.*

Note the sensitive wording: Bela's getting "a featured spot"; Boris has "the lead." At any rate, Ulmer has created a meaty role for Lugosi: Dr. Vitus Werdegast, the tragic hero of *The Black Cat*. The actor probably won't be aware of the full impact of his part until he returns to Hollywood and sees the final script, but meanwhile, Universal has sweetened the offer with options for two more films: *Dracula's Daughter* and *The Suicide Club*.

The wheels are now in motion for the shooting of *The Black Cat*, spiked with incest, necrophilia, sexual perversity, and insanity – and headlined by the two superstars of Hollywood horror. The news is sensational, and spreads fast.

Tuesday, February 13: Columnist Jimmy Starr informs readers in *The Los Angeles Evening Herald Express*:

Here's fair warning... Prepare your spines..."Dracula" (Bela Lugosi) and "Frankenstein" (Boris Karloff) are to be co-starred by Universal in The Black Cat, *Edgar Allan Poe's noted mystery... Can you imagine Dracula trying to outscare Frankenstein? Or vice versa? That will be just DUCKY!*

Meanwhile, other Universal and horror-related events:

Thursday, February 15: James Whale, Universal's director of *Frankenstein*, *The Old Dark House*, and *The Invisible Man*, arrives on the *Europa* in New York City after a 12-week vacation in his native England. He brings another Karloff vehicle: *A Trip to Mars*, scripted by R.C. Sherriff. (It's never produced.)

Also on February 15: Carl Laemmle, Sr. leaves New York for Hollywood, but Junior remains in Manhattan, attending tonight's premiere of the play *Queer People*. The novel by Carroll and Garrett Graham had been a sensation in Hollywood, a thinly-veiled lampoon of various cinema names, some allegedly based on personages at Universal City. The play features two orgy scenes and a murder. Junior, spooked, hopes to acquire the film rights from Howard Hughes, thereby controlling the movie and saving his studio any humiliation. There's no need – the play's a flop.

By the way, playing a suicide in *Queer People*: Dwight Frye, the fly-eating Renfield in *Dracula* and hunchbacked Fritz in *Frankenstein*.

Friday, February 16: *The Lost Patrol* opens at Los Angeles' RKO-Hillstreet Theatre, where it will shatter attendance records. Karloff's stock soars higher.

Saturday, February 17: *The Hollywood Reporter* reports that Universal has tested Erin O'Brien Moore "for one of the leading roles" in *The Black Cat*. The actress is from the Broadway stage and new in Hollywood. Edgar Ulmer is very particular about the casting of the leading lady, for a very particular reason.

CHAPTER 6

JOEN

I'd describe my mother as a femme fatale – very attractive to men. She was a "Fanchonette," one of the Fanchon and Marco dancers who danced at the Paramount Theatre in Los Angeles and quite a lot of other places, including Silent movies. She was a tiny little woman, 5' tall, with very dark hair and almost black eyes, a great beauty, known for her gorgeous legs.

Joen Mitchell, Edgar Ulmer's daughter by an early marriage.

Joen Warner, dancer, leg double, and Edgar Ulmer's first wife. Ulmer would name the heroine of The Black Cat *after her.*
Courtesy of her daughter, Joen Mitchell

After her father's death in 1972, Arianne Ulmer sought a half-sister via an early marriage her father rarely discussed. Ironically, the sister found *her* twenty-five years later after reading Peter Bogdanovich's 1997 collection of director profiles and interviews, *Who the Devil Made It* (which reprinted his Ulmer interview from *Kings of the B's*). The first wife's name was Joen Warner, and she'd wed Ulmer at the Riverside Mission August 21, 1926. Edgar and Joen honeymooned at Lake Arrowhead, where Ulmer worked with F.W. Murnau filming *Sunrise*. Intriguingly, Joen resembled Margaret Livingston, *Sunrise's* dark, vampy "Woman from the City."

Their daughter Joen was born December 15, 1929. In 2001, Joen Mitchell (the daughter-in-law of the man who invented the Mitchell camera) spoke with me about her mother Joen, including the fact that she'd been a "leg double" for various Silent stars:

Clara Bow didn't have very pretty legs, and when they shot Clara Bow's legs, those were my mother's legs. Pola Negri was another for whom my mother was a "leg double." I remember her showing me how to do the Charleston – a very mean Charleston! She was a flapper, absolutely.

As Joen Mitchell recalls, her parents were divorced "by the time I was three or four years old," which would have been shortly before *The Black Cat*. The unhappy marriage apparently left lasting scars on both man and wife. Her mother eventually married a man from rural Montana ("very different from my father," says Joen) and died in 1988. Joen met Edgar Ulmer only once, when she was 17. ("My mother had to make contact with my father as part of a financial settlement for past child support, and he wanted to see me.") By the way, Joen Mitchell has seen *The Black Cat*. Her impression?

"It gave me the creeps," she laughs. "I don't like creepy things. I'm *anti*-scary, creepy things!"

Surely it was no coincidence that Ulmer named the heroine of *The Black Cat*, who spends most of the film screaming and fainting and nearly ends up the sacrifice of a lunatic satanic high priest...Joan. Meanwhile, Peter Ruric, working with Ulmer on the script, names the hero, an author of mysteries...Peter.

Tuesday, February 20, 1934: "Lugosi Arrives Today," headlines *The Hollywood Reporter*:

Bela Lugosi gets in today by train from New York to start work in Edgar Allan Poe's The Black Cat, *which goes into production next Saturday. Boris Karloff has the top spot...*

Wednesday, February 21: Junior Laemmle heads back from New York to California by train, escaping the blizzards that are plaguing the east.

Also on February 21: *The Hollywood Reporter*, that regularly places film land folk in "the Dog House" for saying or doing something silly, bestows the honor on Eph Asher, executive producer of *The Black Cat* (as he'd been on most of the Universal horror classics). Asher made it into the Dog House "for alibiing a scratched nose by claiming he fell out of bed after reading the script of *The Black Cat*."

Shirley Kassler Ulmer had a different memory of Asher: He'd meet Ulmer for story conferences while sitting on the toilet. "There'd be Asher," Shirley laughed, "having a 'b.m.,' holding up the script and saying to Edgar, 'I've read it – and I think it's *great*!'"

Thursday, February 22: 20th Century's *House of Rothschild* previews at the Westwood Village Theatre. The star is George Arliss, and Boris Karloff plays the anti-Semitic Count Ledrantz. Karloff had made the epic on loan to 20th Century in late 1933. Loretta Young and Robert Young are the romantic leads and the finale is in Technicolor. "ROTHSCHILD A WINNER" headlines *The Hollywood Reporter* the next morning, calling the film "about the most important money picture we have seen during the past two years" and noting Karloff "a standout."

Friday, February 23: "Snow Stops Lugosi," headlines *The Hollywood Reporter*, which was apparently premature in its February 20 announcement that Bela was back in Hollywood. The notice reads:

Bela Lugosi, who is driving out here for his role in The Black Cat, *ran into a snowstorm in Texas and will not arrive until the early part of next week. Picture has been shoved back on the schedule and will not start until the middle of next week.*

Bela didn't drive, so this report indicates that Lillian was driving as they made their way west through the bitter weather. Meanwhile, Ulmer still hasn't decided whether to cast Erin O'Brien Moore as Joan, or pursue other possibilities. Nor has he cast the romantic leading man. The film, originally set to start shooting the next day, Saturday the 24th, is nowhere near ready.

Saturday, February 24: *Variety* notes that "Jacqueline Wells, Maureen O'Sullivan and Erin O'Brien Moore are being considered for the fem lead in *Black Cat* at Universal." The casting of Ms. O'Sullivan seems a pipe dream, as she's a major MGM attraction, currently cavorting in her loincloth in *Tarzan and his Mate*; it seems doubtful Metro will loan her out. Ms. O'Brien Moore and Ms. Wells, the latter having recently co-starred with W.C. Fields in Paramount's *Tillie and Gus* (1933), appear to be the top contenders.

Meanwhile, Universal has sent the script for *The Black Cat* to Joseph Breen, head of the Production Code. Breen is hell-bent on putting teeth into the hitherto-lax Code, hell-bent on saving the country from Hollywood, and saving Hollywood from itself.

Will Joseph Ignatius Breen, a devout Roman Catholic, approve *The Black Cat*'s Modern Lucifer and his posse?

CHAPTER 7

HOLLYWOOD PAGANISM

Sexual perversion is rampant, and any number of our prominent stars and directors are perverts.

Joseph Breen, letter to Will H. Hays, 1933.

Will H. Hays, former U.S. Postmaster General (1921-1922) and the first enforcer of the Production Code

Joseph Ignatius Breen, determined to put teeth into the Production Code

Monday, February 26: Eph Asher, Peter Ruric and Edgar Ulmer apparently pour on the charm this morning as they meet with Joe Breen. The censor czar, who has decried the "paganism" of Hollywood, surprisingly decrees that *The Black Cat* script "suggests no difficulty, from the standpoint of our Production code."

Perhaps he believes this horror show is not to be taken too seriously. Nevertheless, in a letter written to Universal on February 26, after the meeting, Breen does come on strong on two big points:

The major difficulty on this score is indicated by the gruesomeness, which is suggested by the script, dealing with

the scenes of the action of skinning a man alive. It is our understanding that you propose to suggest this merely by shadow or silhouette, but as we suggested this morning, this particular phase of your production will have to be handled with great care, lest it become too gruesome or revolting.

The second major difficulty is suggested by the several sequences in which the script calls for a cat to be killed. Mr. Ulmer understands, I think, that any definite suggestion of cruelty to animals will invite considerable trouble, both for your studio and this Association.

Additionally, Breen listed in his letter 20 (!) points, which the Universal trio had agreed that morning would "be taken care of":

- *Sequence A-7: Care should be taken with the performance of the photographer to avert any suggestion of homosexuality.*
- *Sequence B-5: It might be wise to change this derogatory reference to Czech Slovakians as people who devour the young.*

- *Sequence B-43: This scene of the man anxiously waiting in front of the lavatory and following the girl when she comes out will probably be deleted by several censor boards.*

- *Sequence D-21: This action of the cat licking blood on Joan's shoulder will likely be cut. This also applies to the brutal killing of the cat which follows.*

- *Sequence E-6: This scene of a man in bed with a nude woman and all it implies should be omitted.*

- *Sequence E-19: In Werdegast's speech, "...I mean you always <u>wanted</u> her," it would be advisable to change the underlined word.*

- *Sequence E-25: The killing of the cat will probably be cut by a number of the censor boards.*

- *Sequence F-3: This scene of the corpse of a young girl suspended in a glass coffin, as well as the other scenes of the other corpse, is rather gruesome and is open to serious objection.*

- *Sequence F-11: The insidious suggestion of the caress in this scene should be omitted.*

- *Sequence G-5: Care should be taken that Werdegast's interest in Joan when he examines her be not too suggestive.*

- *Sequence G-18: Care should be taken where Joan's head and shoulders appear from the shower to prevent any suggestion of indecent exposure. Also, it might be well to omit the action of Peter pressing against the bathroom door.*

- *Sequence H-26: The objection to the appearance of a corpse appears here.*

- *Sequence H-32: In introducing the guests, it would be well to avoid any suggestion of German nationality in presenting these people. Also, in the scene, care should be taken to avoid any suggestion of homosexuality or perversion of any of the characters.*

- *Sequences I-24 and 34: Here again applies the objection to the corpse.*
- *Sequence I-36: Use of the inverted cross here is definitely inadvisable.*

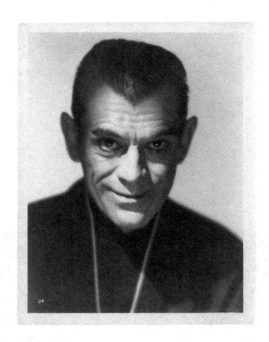

- *Throughout this celebration of the Black Mass of Poelzig's rituals, care should be taken to avoid any suggestion of a parody on any church ceremony.*

- *Sequence I-44: In this scene there should be no suggestion of the performance of any sexual rite.*

- *Sequence J-6: Care should be taken to keep the appearance of this set from being too gruesome.*

- *Sequences J-16, 17, 18, 19, 26 and 30: These scenes of skinning a man alive are too brutal and gruesome and some change should be made to bring them in conformance under the code. This entire sequence is a very dangerous one and it would be advisable for us to discuss them thoroughly before any other preparation is made.*

- *Sequence J-36: The implication of sexual intimacy in this scene should be eliminated.*

Ulmer's response? He cuts all of sequence A, which presented the wedding of Peter Alison and Joan in a cathedral, and the presumably homosexual photographer. He also changes the line about Czech Slovakians eating their young to, "Tasmanians eat their young." (The line won't appear in the film anyway.) Otherwise, he blithely ignores <u>virtually every one</u> of the other 18 suggestions.

Meanwhile, Junior Laemmle is back from New York, eager to start *The Black Cat*. Ulmer proceeds with casting the film, filling three of the major roles on the same day.

CHAPTER 8

A Hyper-Hero, a "Hyper-Virgin," and "The Virgin Mary"

Manners in 'Cat'
David Manners goes to Universal for The Black Cat *starting Wednesday. He'll have the juve romantic lead.*
Variety, *February 27, 1934*

A candid shot of David Manners with Colin Clive, taken at Tiffany Studios, Hollywood, during the shooting of "Journey's End" (1930).
Clive would play Henry Frankenstein in "Frankenstein" (1931) and "Bride of Frankenstein" (1935).

Girls In 'Black Cat'

"Added to the cast of Universal's Black Cat *chiller are* Jacqueline Wells *and* Lucille Lund, *latter the All American Girl Universal brought out from Northwestern University for her maiden screen role in* Saturday's Millions.
"Starting Friday." – Variety, *February 27, 1934*

David Manners was the top romantic hero of Horror's Golden Age.

He had made his film debut in *Journey's End* (Tiffany, 1930). A personal discovery of James Whale, he'd played

Raleigh, who climactically dies in the arms of Colin Clive's Captain Stanhope. A contract had followed with Warners/First National, where he became the onscreen boy-toy for many a high-powered actress. Nevertheless, he found stardom decidedly uncomfortable.

"Wherever I went, I always seemed to be 'on-show,'" Manners would tell this author in 1976. "I didn't feel free."

He's a hypersensitive man. Stark memories of Colin Clive's harrowing, real-life Jekyll/Hyde alcoholism on

Journey's End haunt him. He adored many of his leading ladies – Barbara Stanwyck, Katharine Hepburn, and especially *Dracula's* Helen Chandler – but had suffered with divas Loretta Young and Kay Francis. He'd bitterly protested Jack L. Warner farming him out at a profit; for example, on *Dracula*, Warner loaned Manners to Universal at $500 per week, while Manners received his usual $300 per week. When Manners eventually demanded full pay for future loan-outs, Warner exploded.

"Go to Hell!" roared Warner, who dropped Manners from the studio.

As a freelancer, he's acted with Karloff in *The Mummy* and with Lugosi in *The Death Kiss*. Audiences in 1933 had seen him co-starring with Gloria Stuart, Claudette Colbert and Carole Lombard. He had never liked horror films and signs for *The Black Cat* with considerable reluctance. In just two years, he'll retire from Hollywood forever.

Jacqueline Wells, a child actress in Silents, is now an all-purpose ingénue – everything from Laurel and Hardy's *Any Old Port* (1932), to Ophelia in the Pasadena Playhouse's 1933 revival of *Hamlet*, to Buster Crabbe's leading lady (with Harlow-esque platinum hair) in Principal's 12-chapter serial *Tarzan the Fearless*.

"I spent most of my time in *Tarzan the Fearless* lying in a tree!" she laughed during an interview with this author in 1997.

She's back to auburn tresses as Edgar Ulmer selects her to play *The Black Cat's* heroine, Joan Alison, described by the script as "hyper-virginal." When Jacqueline reads the script, and learns she will play High Priest Poelzig's desired sacrifice to Satan, she's both surprised and frightened.

Blonde Lucille Lund had arrived at Universal in July, 1933, having won the studio's "The All-American Girl" contest (1,200 contestants) while attending Northwestern University. The studio awarded her roles in *Saturday's Millions* (1933) and *Horse Play* (1934), but she quickly ran afoul of Junior Laemmle, whom Lucille always referred to as "Little Napoleon." As she told this author in a 1991 interview:

"Little Napoleon" was very small in stature, smiling all the time, and didn't have much oomph as a producer. But he was in charge while I was there (completely!), and he liked girls very much. Including me!

One night at a party, Junior made his play for Lucille,
who loomed over him in her high heels –and refused his advances. The gossip quickly bestows upon her a Universal City nickname: "The Virgin Mary."

Junior's revenge: he'd tossed Lucille into a serial, the 12-chapter *Pirate Treasure*, and threatened to dump her from the studio. However, Ulmer decided to cast Lucille in *The Black Cat* as Karen, the "Scarlet Woman" role of the piece. As he envisions it, Karen has the sensuality and the look of a Siamese cat – and, in her depravity, is stark, raving, and hysterically mad. In fact, Lucille actually wins *two* roles in *The Black Cat*: she will play her own mother as well, also named Karen, a beautifully preserved corpse, lovingly displayed by Karloff's Poelzig, hanging from her long blonde hair in a vertical glass coffin.

For these reasons, and more, *The Black Cat* will be a true nightmare for Lucille Lund.

With the five star roles finally cast as of February 27, Junior and Ulmer decide to start shooting the next day.

Jacqueline Wells won the role of Joan Alison in "The Black Cat". The actress previously had starred in two Universal serials: "Heroes of the West" (under the name Diane Duval, 1932), and "Clancy of the Mounted" (1933). Her hair had been blonde in the latter.

Lucille Lund, winner of the Universal's "The All-American Girl" contest, shows off her long blonde tresses in this publicity shot.

JACQUELINE WELLS in **"THE BLACK CAT"** — A Universal Production PRINTED IN U.S.A.

In early 1932, Lugosi and Karloff had posed for publicity shots at Universal City. Here, Boris threatens Bela—just for laughs.

The Bela Lugosi house, "Castle La Paloma" in Hollywood Hills, below the old HOLLYWOODLAND sign. Bela lived here at the time of The Black Cat.

Lugosi with one of his dogs at above house, which has recently received a major restoration.

CHAPTER 9

The Production Blueprint

FRANKENSTEIN And DRACULA
Together in
THE BLACK CAT

Universal PR material for *The Black Cat*

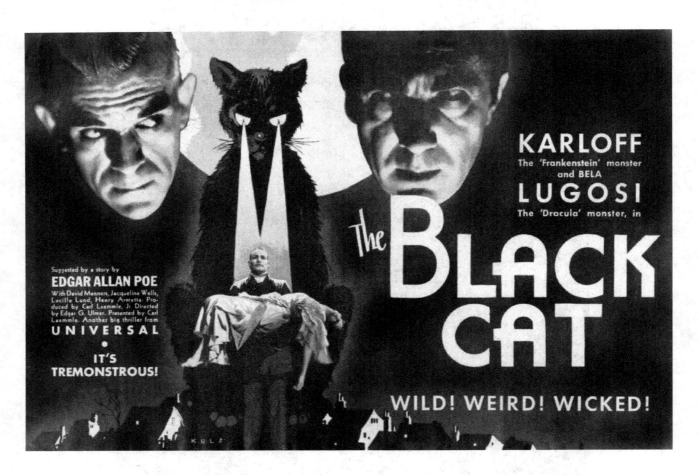

The shooting blueprint for *The Black Cat* reveals intriguing facts and figures:

• The surviving Universal Picture Corporation production estimate for film # 677 reveals a budget of only $91,125.00 – 25% of which is studio overhead. To place this into perspective, the budget of *Dracula* had been $355,050; the budget of *Frankenstein*, $262,007. Also compare this to Universal's big film of 1934, *Imitation of Life*, which will begin shooting in June on a budget of $565,750. In fact, Claudette Colbert, star of *Imitation of Life*, will be set for a salary of $90,277.75. – almost the entire budget of *The Black Cat*.

John Stahl's budgeted fee for directing *Imitation of Life*: $60,000.

• Universal's "Picture Talent" estimate for *The Black Cat* sets Boris Karloff for the role of Poelzig at a guaranteed "flat fee" of $7,500. Apart from this, the studio offers a special treat: having been proclaimed as "KARLOFF the Uncanny" on posters for *The Mummy*, Boris will have top billing in *The Black Cat*, on both posters *and* the screen, as KARLOFF.

• Second-billed Bela Lugosi, as Werdegast, is guaranteed a salary less than half of Karloff's – three weeks' work at a rate of $1,000 per week.

• Ulmer's fee as director is only $900 for the entire picture.

As for the three other major players in *The Black Cat*:

• David Manners, as Peter Alison, originally secures a better deal than Bela: $1,250 per week for two-and-half weeks' work, for a total of $3,125.

• Jacqueline Wells, as Joan, signs on for $300 per week and a guaranteed $900.

• Lucille Lund, as Karen, joins the show for one week at $150 per week.

As for the featured players:

• Harry Cording, heavy, balding and mustached, signs as Thamal, Werdegast's mute, giant servant, for $200 per week and two-and-a-half weeks' work. Cording will become a fixture at Universal, in such horrors as 1939's *Son of Frankenstein* and 1941's *The Wolf Man*.

• Egon Brecher, who'd played such roles as Captain Hook in Eva Le Gallienne's then recently-disbanded Civic Repertory Theatre, portrays Poelzig's sinister Major-domo, on a $500 per week contract for two weeks and one day's work.

• Henry Armetta and Albert Conti sign on as the bickering Sergeant and Lieutenant, who provide *The Black Cat* its one fleeting vignette of comic relief. Armetta's and Conti's salaries, respectively: $150 and $125 for the film.

• Anna Duncan, stepdaughter of dancer Isadora Duncan, contracts to play the Poelzig maid, set at $125 per week and two weeks' work. Early publicity claims Ms. Duncan will dance *The Appasionata* in *The Black Cat*; she won't.

Also, Ulmer is fortunate in his cinematographer: the brilliant (but tragically alcoholic) John J. Mescall, who the following year will be James Whale's cameraman on *Bride of Frankenstein*.

With blizzards still whirling through the east, wild and wicked weather appropriately hits Hollywood. Karloff weathers the storms at Toluca Lake. Lugosi has returned to his cliffside house in the Hills, 2835 Westshire Drive, below the HOLLYWOODLAND sign, a domain with a magnificent view and known 80 years later as "Castle La Paloma." Meanwhile, Shirley Kassler Alexander – who'd fallen in love with Edgar Ulmer – is delighted to get work on *The Black Cat* as an assistant to the script girl.

Wednesday, February 28: A member of Joseph Breen's staff reviews the script for *The Black Cat* and sends this inter-office memorandum to Breen:

This new script has cut the first sequence of the original script, the wedding scene. Except for that, I find no appreciable change.

In fact, the only changes I find is the elimination of the reference to Czech Slovakians and the description of the inverted cross, although a cross of some type is still used.

As for the skinning alive scenes, they remain unchanged.

For the time being, Joe Breen lets it slide. Meanwhile, on this day, Edgar G. Ulmer begins shooting *The Black Cat*.

CHAPTER 10

ACT I

Of what use are all these melodramatic gestures?

Boris Karloff as Poelzig, *The Black Cat.*

The newlyweds Jacqueline Wells and David Manners (the Alisons) in their train compartment.

The Orient Express.

The Black Cat opens in a dark, gloomy train depot with a flourish of Liszt's "Hungarian Rhapsody." Universal lifts the atmospheric opening from the British film *Rome Express* (1932), starring Conrad Veidt. Snug in Compartment F, Car 96 sit our newlyweds: David Manners as Peter and Jacqueline Wells as Joan. But "a terrible mistake" has happened – space has been sold in their compartment to a gentleman.

"Do please forgive this intrusion," intones Bela Lugosi's Dr. Vitus Werdegast.

"Oh, he looked beautiful in that!" Lillian Lugosi once sighed about her husband in *The Black Cat.* Bela's widow Hope told me that Bela's favorite of all his films was *The Black Cat* because he was so handsome in it. In fact, in January of 1956, six months before he died, Bela went to see a revival of *The Black Cat* in Los Angeles.

"...Lugosi *screams* out," remembered Hope, "so everybody can turn around and see who he is – "OH, WHAT A HANDSOME BASTARD I WAS!"

With Werdegast's "intrusion," *The Black Cat* starts its wild, sexually aberrant course. And as Bela, after ominously announcing his intent to "visit an old friend," opens the shutter and looks out into the night, his own reflection, diabolical in the dark and shrouded with smoke from the train, glares back at him. Accompanying this shot in the released film: Liszt's brooding *Tasso* - Werdegast's leitmotif.

The train races through the stormy night, itself diabolical with its blazing furnace and billowing smoke. The strains of Tchaikovsky's *Romeo and Juliet* serve as the Alisons' theme. Peter awakens to find Werdegast gently stroking the hair of his sleeping wife. Bela movingly builds a passionate monologue:

I beg your indulgence, my friend. Eighteen years ago I left a girl – so like your lovely wife – to go to war. Kaiser and country, you know. She was my wife. Have you ever heard of – Kurgaal? It is a prison below Omsk on Lake Baikal. Many men have gone there. Few have returned. I have returned. After fifteen years – I have returned!

Was Bela thinking of his own Word War I war wounds? Whatever his "method," the delivery here has wonderful intensity. Edgar Ulmer carefully kept Bela in check.

"You had to cut away from Lugosi continuously," Ulmer told Bogdanovich, "to cut him down. He nearly ate my set up!"

2:00 a.m. The train arrives at stormy Visegrad – actually the Universal back lot, with rain machines and 75 "Midnite Meals" catered for the late night shoot. Werdegast and the Alisons board a bus, accompanied by Vitus's servant, Thamal, a giant mute, reminiscent of the Golem. Harry Cording well suits the role. In heralding thunder and lightning, the bus rolls off into the Carpathian Mountains.

A crash. Jacqueline Wells screams and faints for the first time in the movie. There, atop a Carpathian crag, introduced with a blast of Liszt's *The Rakoczy March*, looming over a graveyard with storm clouds racing in the night sky, is Fort Marmaros.

It's Hell on a mountaintop... the lair of Hjalmar Poelzig.

Fort Marmaros

"It was very, very much out of my Bauhaus period," said Ulmer of Fort Marmaros. It's a modernistic Art-Deco glass and marble masterwork, sleekly sinister and totally unique from the Gothic creations usually featured in Universal horror. Ulmer designed Fort Marmaros's great hall, with its sinuous staircase and *avant-garde* arches, for $3,700, plus $1,000 worth of *objet d'art* props.

The stranded foursome enter Marmaros, Thamal carrying the unconscious Joan, accompanied by Chopin's Second *Piano Prelude* and admitted by Egon Brecher's gnarled Majordomo, the bald actor wearing a $100-made-to-order, beetle-browed hairpiece so bad one imagines it was intentionally to appear a toupee. Bela briskly demands a place to dress the lady's injury and the Majordomo announces the visitors via intercom. The shooting script notes the remarkably sensual effect as we see the Poelzig bedroom – the "very large low square bed," the sheets of "smoke-colored gauze" descending around it:

As the CAMERA approaches the bed the upper part of a man's body rises slowly, as if pulled by wires, to a sitting position. In rising, one arm sweeps backward and covers with a gauze thin sheet the nude body of a woman. We are not shown her nudity but know it from the curve of her body under the thin sheet...

The rising of Poelzig, "as if pulled by wires," is also an Ulmer homage: to the way Murnau's vampire rises in *Nosferatu*. Werdegast tends to the still unconscious Joan; Peter winces as the psychiatrist injects a narcotic. *The Black Cat* then leaps into the wildly theatrical as the door opens...

There stands KARLOFF's Poelzig – a modern Lucifer, strikingly festooned in satanic hairdo and black robe and heralded by a crash of *Sonata in B Minor* by Liszt – "The Devil Sonata" itself! "The earthly incarnation of Satan" is how the shooting script all-hails Poelzig. The magnificent eyes ravage the sleeping Joan as Ulmer treats Karloff's Prince of Darkness to a richly reverential entrance, John J. Mescall's camera virtually genuflecting before him. High Priest Poelzig will be Boris's most sly, perverse, feline performance; indeed, the actor prowls through *The Black Cat* like...well, a black cat. Karloff, in the course of the film, also suggests a snake, a fox, a wolf, and a king vulture — he's not only Lucifer, but Lucifer's zoo.

On the set, "Dear Boris" is a devil too, as well as a pussycat. As Ulmer will remember:

...Karloff was a very charming man...Very charming. And he never took himself seriously. My biggest job was to keep him in the part, because he laughed at himself...One of the nicest scenes I had with him, he lies in bed next to the daughter of

Lugosi, and the young couple rings down at the door, and he gets up and you see him the first time in costume, in that modernistic set...he got into bed, we got ready to shoot, and he got up, he turned to the camera, after he put his shoes on, and said, "Boo!"

Every time I had him come in by the door, he would open the door and say, "Here comes the heavy..." He was a very, very lovely man...a very fine actor. Five star. As you know, he lisped – but the way he used that lisp – he knew exactly how to overcome the handicap.

As for Lucille Lund, who'd been sharing the bed with Karloff in what she called the "Glamour Boudoir scene"...in 1991, she was a beautiful, gracious widow, living on a Malibu hill with a magnificent view of the Pacific. She had several happy memories of *The Black Cat*, primarily due to its star.

"Karloff was darling," said Lucille. "He was so funny!" As she reminisced:

Oh, Boris Karloff was a very charming, British gentleman – a delight! He looked ferocious, but he had a little lisp, so he didn't sound like he looked at all! Boris would stand around, singing little Cockney ditties, like,

"Don't hand me into another,
Because I am about to become a mother" –

Funny little things. They were a little off-color, but really cute! Every day, at four o'clock, I don't care how busy the scene was, Karloff stopped for tea. And nobody seemed to care, because that was the way he wanted it. Very cute! Very nice!

I have all kind of remembrances about The Black Cat, but mainly I remember very fondly Boris, who was the most delightful, charming man you could ever meet – just altogether lovely.

I even enjoyed the scene where I ended up in the boudoir with Boris. He didn't look bad at all, actually!

There was an oddity about this episode, as Lucille remembered:

We did the "Glamour Boudoir scene "– and the thing that struck me as a little peculiar, right off the bat, was that not much of me showed under this satin sheet. But Ulmer had made for me, especially, a little tiny one-piece bathing suit – made out of the sheerest net. Nothing underneath it! It could have been flesh-colored crepe, or something that wasn't see-through, but he wanted it that way.

You'll notice I'm well under the sheet in The Black Cat.

Well, if you'd been in the "thing" I had on, you would have pulled the sheet up too!

"You sold Marmaros to the Russians," sneers Bela. "...The murderer of 10,000 men returns to the place of his crime!" Bela stands delivering his juicy dialogue. Although Boris sits silently, he's strangely dominant – his Satanist perversely flanked by what appear to be Easter lilies.

"I was taken prisoner," continues Bela, his face and tone haunted. "To Kurgaal... where the soul is killed – slowly. Fifteen years I've rotted in the darkness – waited. Not to kill you – to kill your soul..." And then, demanding: "Where is my wife, Karen? And my daughter?"

"Vitus," says Boris, dramatically rising, "you are mad!"

The leer on Karloff's face becomes a sick smile - Manners has entered the study. The Majordomo gets Peter a whiskey and Poelzig turns on his 1934 state-of-the-art radio, offering a bit of Schubert's *Unfinished Symphony*.

"Engineer Poelzig is one of Austria's greatest architects," says Bela.

"And Dr. Werdegast," smiles Boris, in a line that taxes his lisp to the limit, "is one of Hungary's greatest psychiatrists."

Manners melodramatically whispers that he's an author of "Mysteries!" and Bela proposes a toast. "To you, my friend. To your charming wife... and to Love!"

A black cat appears in the doorway.

For all the ballyhoo of Universal's Black Cat Contest, the production records reveal a dispatch to the studio ranch, engaging "1 Special Black Cat" for two weeks' work and a Depression salary of $200. Fifty dollars was allotted for "additional cats," perhaps foreseeing prizewinners selected on that gala day on the back lot. Certainly, it was good money in 1934 for an animal.

"In those days," said Shirley Kassler Ulmer, "I was making $50 a week, and considered *very* highly paid!"

At the sight of the cat, all of Werdegast's continental charm withers; the anguished soul drops his glass, grabs a knife and hurls it fatally at the cat. Bela's Vitus tries to recover as Boris's Hjalmar grins and slinks around him, enjoying his "old friend's" fit. Karloff recalled Lugosi later accused him of scene-stealing; this perhaps was one of those instances. At any rate, both stars are superb in this *outré* episode.

"Lugosi was afraid of cats," Hope Lugosi told the *Enquirer* in 1957. "He hated them. Now I have a black cat sitting in front of his painting. If he knew that he'd die all over again."

Meanwhile, the Black Cat and KARLOFF aren't the only ones slinking. So is Jacqueline Wells, who enters in her negligee, suddenly a sexpot, apparently possessed by the evil spirit of the now-dead cat: "... There is something distinctly feline in her expression, in the way she moves...," says the script. "You are frightened, Doctor?" she asks Werdegast, with a hint of the "faintly malicious smile" the script calls for, and then vamps Boris. Clearly enjoying the evil metamorphosis, he takes her hand, sensually kisses it, and purrs:

You must be indulgent of Dr. Werdegast's weakness. He is the unfortunate victim of one of the commoner phobias, but in an extreme form. He has an intense and all-consuming horror – of cats!

As Karloff lisps Lugosi's little secret in his oh-so-catty-way, his eyes roll and his mouth smiles and curls in a delivery that makes the line sexy, sinister, and sacrilegious, all at once!

Jacqueline Wells, later known as Julie Bishop, long and lavishly retired, living in a cliffside Mendocino house with a view of the Pacific, told me in 1997:

The Black Cat was a little scary – getting used to the kind of things we were shooting! I'd never been in a movie like that, you know. I hadn't been in too many at that point, anyway. But I'd never been in anything that was so wild! And I thought, "This is a junk movie," and (laughing) "It's not a 'B,' it's a 'C or a 'D'"! I remember especially the first few days of production that I felt, "Oh, what have I gotten into! Look what I have to do!"

Then I got to know Boris.

I had always admired Boris's work – the parts he played – Oooh! But I was not at all prepared for Boris Karloff, the man. It was difficult to associate the horror performances I had seen with this extremely bright, beautifully educated man, every inch the gentleman.

Boris was such a lovely person, and we got along so well! I did with the rest of the cast, too. But Boris and I just stayed and talked in between scenes and seemed to understand each other; he sort of "comforted" me on this horror picture that actually frightened me. We just sat and talked, the days went

by fast and I was delighted with this man, because he was just such a gentleman. He was nice to everybody. And he was such a fine actor, it was a joy to work with him.

I have been fortunate, working with a great many excellent male stars, and I have thoroughly appreciated each of them. But none of them have I respected more than Boris – both as an actor, and a gentleman.

The leading lady also found Bela Lugosi charming:

Lugosi was a delight, kind and considerate to work with. I liked him very much. But we didn't visit between scenes. He was very serious and I just didn't get as well-acquainted with him as I did with Boris.

The possessed Joan sashays to Peter, giving David Manners the most passionate kiss he ever received in the movies. The camera watches it voyeuristically from beneath the robed sleeve of Poelzig, who, his own passion aroused by the sight of the kiss, grasps a statue of a nude woman atop his desk. As Joan kisses Peter, John Mescall's camera sensually focuses back and forth from the lovers' kiss to the clutching arm – a remarkable effect.

The film plays on, the two stars savoring their baroque dialogue.

""Supernatural – perhaps," intones Bela's Werdegast. "Baloney – perhaps not. There are many things – under the sun!"

"...the Black Cat is deathless," meows Karloff's Poelzig. "Deathless as Evil!"

The night proceeds. Poelzig takes Werdegast deep into the hellish, dynamite-fraught cellars of Fort Marmaros. It's here where Poelzig keeps his special trophy. Hanging from her long, blonde, beehive hair in a vertical, Snow White style crystal coffin is the cadaver of Karen, the ex-wife of Werdegast and Poelzig – played by Lucille Lund.

Lucille Lund is truly one of the sensations of *The Black Cat*. Later in the film, in full bloom as the living Karen in cascading blonde hair and sexy black negligee, she evokes Rapunzel, after a shopping spree at Frederick's of Hollywood. She gives off the aura of a depraved angel. Arianne Ulmer told me:

My father loved angels – very baroque angels – and everything that was Gothic. Although he was Jewish, he was brought up in Austria, a Catholic country, and taught by Jesuits. He loved cathedrals – I remember he took me to Christmas Midnight Mass in Rome when I was 10 or 11. He adored Bach and religious music, and this was very important to him. Yes, the Lucille Lund look in The Black Cat – she looks like a Christmas angel. Absolutely.

There hangs Lucille, looming above Karloff and Lugosi, playing dead. Having suffered sexual harassment from Junior Laemmle, Lucille now faces it again – from Edgar Ulmer. It had started with her fishnet lingerie in the "Glamour Boudoir" scene, and proceeded to Sardi's restaurant in Hollywood, one night, where Ulmer had proposed that she became his lover. "We would be a combination like Dietrich and Von Sternberg," he promised. Lucille said no thanks.

"That's when the horror started," said Lucille Lund. "And it was not in the script, believe me!"

It was, ironically, in this horrific episode that Lucille truly suffered:

Do you remember that glass coffin that stood end-on-end? They had a big hook at the top and they twisted my very long hair (all my own hair) around that hook, so it looked like it was standing straight up. Then they had a little contraption – sort of like a pair of canvas panties that they put me in, that went up under my long robes; these were suspended by wires so I was lifted, and my feet were dangling, and it appeared I was hanging from my hair. I was virtually hanging in that little "panty," and there was no way I could get out of that glass coffin unless somebody lifted me out and took me out.

So, on this day, as I hung in the "panty," in the coffin, Ulmer said, "Cut! Everybody go to lunch!" Well, he left me there – hanging – for one hour! I couldn't get out! I couldn't do anything!...Evidently, Ulmer told somebody to leave me there... He turned out to be very sadistic!...It was a harrowing experience...

Surely, had Boris and Bela – both great gentlemen, and both founders of the Screen Actors Guild – had any idea of what Lucille was facing, they'd have aggressively intervened. But Lucille, shocked and ashamed, did what most college-age girls would have done in 1934: she kept quiet, fearing and wondering when and how Ulmer would strike next. She'd soon find out.

Werdegast sees his wife Karen, posed hanging in her casket. Karloff illuminates the coffin; with a strange, graceful, almost balletic gesture, he lovingly touches the glass casket and looks up at the beautifully preserved body. "I have cared for her tenderly and well," says Poelzig, claiming she died of pneumonia. He also says that Werdegast's daughter is dead.

Bela never looked so handsome in the movies as he does in this close-up, teary-eyed and mournfully lovesick at the sight of his violated Karen. "And why is she..." asks Bela heartbreakingly, "...why is she... like this?"

"Is she not beautiful?" hisses Boris. "I wanted to have her beauty, always. I loved her *too,* Vitus."

"Lies! All lies, Hjalmar! You killed her! You killed her, as I am about to kill you!" Werdegast draws his pistol – and the alive-again black cat runs into the scene. With a scream, Werdegast falls back with his pistol, crashing into the glass gun chart.

Beethoven's *Seventh Symphony* begins, like a hallowed hymn for lost souls. Mescall's enchanted camera begins a tour of the cellars, up the twisting staircase, as if we, the audience, are there ourselves. Karloff's ghostly, disembodied voice beautifully speaks *The Black Cat's* most memorably sinister soliloquy:

Come, Vitus. Are we men or are we children? Of what use are all these melodramatic gestures? You say your soul was killed, and that you have been dead all these years. And what of me? Did we not both die here in Marmaros, fifteen years ago? Are we any the less victims of the war than those whose bodies were torn asunder? Are we not both – the living dead? And now you come to me – playing at being an avenging angel – childishly thirsting for my blood...

Poelzig shows Werdegast to his room and returns to the "glamour boudoir." The blonde sylph in the bed awakens. We hear Brahms' *Sapphic Ode,* Karen's theme, and we see Lucille Lund again, the living Karen, her blonde hair cascading over the pillow, the satin sheet covering her Ulmer-designed fishnet. Boris slides into the Pre-Code bed with her. "You are the very core and meaning of my life," says Poelzig. "No one shall take you from me. Not even Vitus. Not even your *father.*"

But Poelzig's thoughts also embrace Joan. And the High Priest of Satan opens his book, *Rites of Lucifer,* and reads silently:

In the night, in the dark of the moon, the High Priest assembles his Disciples for the sacrifice. The chosen maiden is garbed in white...

CHAPTER 11

INTERMISSION

Tea time. Lugosi often complained about Karloff's daily 4:00 p.m. tea breaks, although Boris invited Bela to relax with him.

Bela joins in, at least for the photographers.

All is NOT quiet on the western front...shades of those Kentucky mountaineers – another feud has BUSTED loose in Hollywood! This time it's between a couple of chill getters and mystery co-stars, Boris ("Frankenstein") Karloff and Bela ("Dracula") Lugosi, assigned spooky roles in Universal's The Black Cat...

Jimmy Starr, *Los Angeles Evening Herald Express,* March 5, 1934.

The "Twin Titans of Terror" are the talk of Universal City.

Throughout the shoot, the PR boys will flock to the set of *The Black Cat,* shooting candids. They pose Boris on a ladder looking down at Bela, who defies superstition by sitting under it. Every day there is the 4:00 p.m. tea break, Karloff's special treat, for which Universal provides concession. Boris had a sip and a smoke, and

All seems peaceful.

Well...on the fifth day of *The Black Cat's* shooting, the aforementioned Jimmy Starr, gossip monger, regales his readers:

Ordinarily, Boris and Bela are nice, quiet and unassuming chaps, but their jittering roles must have taken effect upon themselves. They are ACTUALLY trying to out-scare each other and have resorted to the ancient Hollywood trick of attempting to steal scenes, resulting in a sneering contest when the cameras aren't in motion. Boris is said to have sneaked in on some of Bela's publicity photographs. And the feud is on – and in earnest!

Thus comes one of *The Black Cat's* most infamous topics: the personal relationship of Karloff and Lugosi. Was this hot hostility, lasting over the decades from

Jimmy Starr in 1934 to *Ed Wood* in 1994 and beyond, genuine?

"We don't stay young and lovely forever!" David Manners had warned me back in 1976, before granting one of his very rare interviews. Manners, 76, trim, classically handsome, and retired from Hollywood for 40 years, was living high in Pacific Palisades, his house overlooking the old Will Rogers Polo Field. He was then writing books on spirituality, and met us in his garden, a portrait of serenity. However, after I brought up his living legend fame in horror films, all visage of inner peace vanished.

"I *hated* doing those things!" winced Manners. "I never *dreamed* they would become classics!"

The Black Cat, however, was a happy memory: "I had a good director in that one," said Manners. "Edgar was most helpful and friendly." Yet the memory also inspired one of his loudest laughs.

Lugosi and Karloff – those two in the same picture!

They weren't very much alike – Karloff, delightful; Lugosi, a mystery and distant. How did they get along? They got along very well, as far as Karloff was concerned. With Lugosi, though, I think there was some jealousy. Lugosi was a big star – in his own mind!

Was there jealousy? 30 years after *The Black Cat*, and eight years after a cruelly humbled Lugosi had been buried in his Dracula cape, Karloff, then 76, delicately addressed the Lugosi situation in a profile in *Films in Review* magazine. The venerable actor was, as writer Robert C. Roman put it, "full of years and some serenity," and living in New York City's "Dakota" apartment house, in lofty quarters that looked out on both the Dakota roof and Central Park (and even had a wood-burning fireplace). Karloff said:

Poor old Bela. It was a strange thing. He was really a shy, sensitive, talented man who had a fine career on the classical stage in Europe. But he made a fatal mistake. He never took the trouble to learn our language. Consequently, he was very suspicious on the set, suspicious of tricks, fearful of what he regarded as scene-stealing. Later, when he realized I didn't go in for such nonsense, we became friends. He had real problems with his speech, and difficulty interpreting lines. I remember he once asked a director what a line of dialogue meant. He spent a great deal of his time with the Hungarian colony in Los Angeles, and this isolated him.

However, while Boris claimed he and Bela eventually became "friends," Lillian Lugosi Donlevy - who drove Bela to Universal and back home again every day – remembered no such relationship. When I asked this low key (and candid) lady way back in 1974 if her husband was ever friendly with Karloff, her response was immediate and dramatic: "No!" She elaborated, giving insight into how Bela had regarded "Dear Boris":

Bela didn't like Karloff; he thought he was "a cold fish." And Karloff was ugly! He lisped! Really, in life, without any makeup or anything, he really was a very unattractive man... Bowed legs...Oh! Everything against him!

Lillian Lugosi Donlevy was a kind lady, so the vehemence of her words is significant. Today, there are quite fanatical Lugosi fans who believe "Dear Boris" was actually a Machiavellian Hollywood villain, a Richard III of Universal City, slyly charming directors and leading ladies, egotistically feathering his own vulture's nest of horror sovereignty, all the while gleefully and guilefully cutting the throat of his competition. They perceive the "Poor Bela" as a special put-down, a calculated insult.

Was Boris Karloff a real-life Monster in the trials and tribulations of Bela Lugosi? Or was Lugosi a "green-eyed monster"?

Shirley Kassler, as assistant script girl, was on *The Black Cat* set every day. She enjoyed a ringside seat at the Boris and Bela dynamic, Edgar directing them with a baton in his hand. She told me in 1988:

Karloff was the "intellect with the lisp" – he was a very well-educated, intelligent guy... The Karloff I first knew at Universal was very posh, dressed immaculately, a bit mysterious, very drawn into himself – unless he met somebody he considered his equal; then you got to know him. I guess I would have never gotten to know him, except for how he opened up to Edgar.

Karloff was a hell of a good actor. Of course, he had this Goddamned lisp! We had a terrible time, because he couldn't say "black cat" – he'd say, "black cath!" But he understood the undercurrents that Ulmer was trying to bring out, with the Black Mass, and so forth.

And Bela didn't.

There was a certain rivalry, because Boris was the "intellect" and Bela was the "performer"...On The Black Cat, Karloff really became the director's "pet," and Lugosi did resent that. You see, when Edgar would start talking in a Kafka-like manner, about music, about psychiatry (Edgar was a Jungian) – things that Lugosi didn't understand – he and Karloff could talk with each other. Karloff and Edgar would go off,

and Edgar would spend evenings with him, and they would have big dissertations....

So, since he couldn't get involved in those conversations on the set, Bela would tell stories – how he had been a hangman back in Hungary! They were weird stories, and I can only wonder how they affected Karloff, who was the perfect gentleman...

You could never call Edgar a "snob"; but in this instance, without meaning to, he might have insulted poor Bela a little bit. Bela couldn't join in the fun Edgar was having with Boris, I guess it made him mad – and, thinking about it now, I don't blame him!

If Bela didn't intellectually understand what Ulmer was talking about on *The Black Cat*, his performance shows that he certainly intuited it *dramatically*. Arianne Ulmer is quick to dispel any impression that Edgar Ulmer was cavalier about Bela's talents:

I don't think that Dad disrespected Lugosi at all. On the contrary, I think he knew he was working with two very good actors, and his big problem was that he could never afford to use them again.

By the way, Bela invited Ulmer and Shirley to dinner at his Hollywood Hills home:

...Edgar, who took me there, had not properly prepared me – and it really was like the worst horror film you ever could imagine! Lugosi had this big painting of himself, in bold, full regalia. His dogs were there. His poor little wife had to serve us, and every time she came in, he insulted her, and screamed at her... I'll never forget it...and I was so scared of him I was really shaking in my pants, too! I wonder if he got a kick out of scaring me...

It was amidst all this angst that a ceremony took place that was incredibly incongruous with the movie it celebrated.

Wednesday, March 14, 1934, 4:00 p.m: It's Universal's "Black Cats Parade." The honorary judges: Karloff and Lugosi. The contestants: Over 300 in number, all the cats vying to win the title role in *The Black Cat* (or so Universal promises). The winning feline that day, judged to be (in the words of the *Los Angeles Examiner*) "the fiercest, weirdest-looking black cat": "Jiggs." Jigg's proud owner: a little girl named Bernice Firestine McGee.

"I am the little girl snuggled up against Boris Karloff," wrote Bernice to me almost 60 years later, seeing a picture from the parade. "I couldn't believe this picture!"

As Bernice remembered the day:

I was only six, but I still remember the kind Boris Karloff. As I recall, Jiggs got a limousine ride! After The Black Cat was finished, Jiggs disappeared quite mysteriously. My mother and I joked about him putting on sunglasses and "going Hollywood" – he just took off!

An interesting sideline: after my picture from the Black Cats Parade appeared in an L.A. newspaper, my family was located by a representative of the Hal Roach Studios. I was a tap dancer even at that young age, and I went on to dance in three Our Gang *comedies. I continued as a dancer in films*

of the '30s, '40s and '50s, and my husband was also a dancer and actor for most of those years. So you see what the Black Cats Parade did for me!

Jewel Firestine, Bernice's mother, confided to me that Bernice won an advantage in the contest by performing impromptu acrobatics ("turning handstands, feet to the sky!"). Jewel beheld Boris and Bela - "They were the first stars I'd ever seen," she recalled in her delightful Texas accent.

Oh, Boris Karloff was just as sweet as he could be! Just so pleasant. He and Bela Lugosi were both really nice. Classy! I remember the little blonde, too – I saw her put her lipstick on with her little finger, and I thought, "I'm gonna try that!" Ohhh, I was just all eyes!

As for the $200 Universal had budgeted for the black cat, Jewel laughed, "Jiggs never got a dime, I never got a dime, and I never asked for a dime!"

There were two runners-up: Evelyn Eady and Bobbie Hayner. *The Los Angeles Examiner* reported the event to have been "a hotly fought contest, including several biting and scratching battles by the felines," and wrote that afterwards, "cream was served to the cats, ice cream to the kiddies, and the party was pronounced 'the cat's meow' by all the proud owners."

And as for the rivalry...in retrospect, one can surely understand Lugosi's concerns. This was Universal, that had exalted Karloff after *Frankenstein* while virtually ignoring Lugosi, even when he was bankrupt and had desperately needed work. KARLOFF had the top-billing by last name only, the exotic costumes, the Lucifer makeup and hairdo, the remarkably theatrical entrances, the 4:00 p.m. tea concession... Doesn't it seem likely the studio will throw him the movie?

And so the shooting continues, Boris loving cricket, Bela favoring soccer, the complex relationship forming, no friendship ever existing, the real-life melodrama only beginning. It would perhaps have been easier for Bela if Boris had been a prima donna, a star who relished his fame as KARLOFF rather than laughing at it. Yet he was such a charming fellow! He was Ulmer's "pet." He was Jacqueline Wells's "comforter." He sang funny songs to Lucille Lund...

Eighty years later, most horror fans agree that Bela Lugosi had deserved so much more from Universal and Hollywood.

The problem was...Boris Karloff deserved no less

"Black Cats Parade," Universal City, California. Boris Karloff, Bela Lugosi, winners Bernice McGee (with her cat "Jiggs"), Evelyn Eady and Bobbie Hayner, and contestants.

CHAPTER 12

ACT II

"Did you ever see an animal skinned, *Hjalmar?"*

Bela Lugosi as Werdegast, *The Black Cat*

Lucifer Crucified: In The Black Cat, *Ulmer provided one of the most perverse images in cinema history. Here, we see Karloff between scenes, half-naked on the rack.*

The second half of The Black Cat is unique in its delirious darkness: a madman's murder of his wife/step-daughter, a Black Mass, the planned ritualistic sacrifice of a virgin, a skinning alive, and a climactic, infernal explosion. Meanwhile, the film itself had become a rivalry between Hollywood's two horror superstars, a son's vendetta against his father, a sexual harassment saga, and a throwing down of the gauntlet to the Production Code.

Joan Alison awakens after her wedding night, *sans* cat-like slinks. Werdegast comes to examine the wound's dressing and learns that Joan remembers nothing after the bus accident. Another Liszt flourish, and Poelzig enters, to enquire as to the health of his "charming guest."

In a wonderfully sinister touch, Karloff turns on profile to leer at his potential sacrifice.

"Poelzig might well be contemplating a very delectable piece of French pastry," notes the script.

The look is so lascivious that Miss Wells needlessly adjusts the bodice of her negligee. However, Boris is not the only one ogling in the original footage. Bela is also staring smolderingly at Joan – for, originally, Werdegast has ascended from the Poelzig cellar partially unhinged and lustful.

Then comes the famous chess game. In the release

print, as Karloff tickles the chess queen, Lugosi challenges him to a game to decide the fate of Joan. "I intend to let her go," says Bela. But this was not the initial dialogue. The original chess game had Poelzig and Werdegast challenging each other for Joan – for Vitus, deranged by the sight of his mummified wife in the cellar, wants Joan for himself.

There follows the comic relief, in *opera bouffe* style, with a Sergeant ("Henry Armetta if possible," noted the script, and it was) and Lieutenant (Albert Conti, who, in Fox's 1930 *Such Men Are Dangerous*, had appeared with Lugosi). They sport capes and accents, and debate (for Peter Alison) the glories of honeymooning in Gombos or Pistyan. Heinz Roemheld will score the scene with a spoof rendition of "The Rakoczy March," appropriately entitled "Hungarian Burlesque".

The chess game goes on. Peter wants to leave; but the car, mysteriously, is out of commission. And the phone is dead.

"You hear that, Vitus?" leers Karloff, his face a Renaissance devil mask. "The phone is dead. Even the *phone* is *dead!*"

Poelzig wins the game. As the Alisons try to leave, Thamal knocks out Peter. Jacqueline Wells screams and faints once again in the movie. Thamal carries the unconscious Joan upstairs to the bedroom, and Thamal and the Majordomo toss Peter into the cellar. Close-ups of Bela, later made in the retakes, will transform his reaction from "morbid interest" to one of sympathy.

The night is approaching. Karloff soulfully plays Bach's *Toccata and Fugue* at his organ. Lugosi, grabbing the key to Joan's bedroom, races upstairs to the ingénue. In one of Bela's best scenes, he warns the terrified Joan, while trying to comfort her. "Definitely underplayed, if you please, M. Lugosi," notes the script, revealing Ulmer's fear of Bela's overacting, calling for "a vague, partly cruel, partly tender, partly impersonal expression:"

Poelzig is a mad beast...Did you ever hear of Satanism, the worship of the Devil, of Evil? Herr Poelzig is the great modern priest of that ancient cult, and tonight, in the dark of the moon, the rites of Lucifer are celebrated. If I am not mistaken, he intends you to play a part in the ritual – a very important part...Dear child...be brave...It is your only chance...!

Karloff's Poelzig about to perform the Black Mass. Lugosi observes. Among the satanists: Michael Mark (back to camera) and Paul Panzer (on profile, next to Lugosi.)

Karloff, Wells, Panzer, Mark and the cross that Joseph Breen had demanded be cut from the film.

Once again, during the three-and-half days of retakes, this speech is altered. The "dear child" section will be added, replacing a scene in which Werdegast's shadow looms over Joan as he almost surrenders to his lust. Poelzig awaits outside the door, and demands the key.

There follows the brief but perversely evocative Karen vignette.

As previously noted, Lucille Lund was to evoke a Siamese cat, permutated by her moral decay as Poelzig's wife/stepdaughter. If Ulmer and Lucille originally went with the cat semblance, Lucille had no memory of it, and Ulmer himself claimed censorship had made a cat-like Karen impossible. Nevertheless, there are some crazy kinks in the originally filmed scene, as Karen – a fetishistic Grand Guignol pin-up, in long blonde hair and flowing black negligee – meets Joan. The black cat precedes her as she enters Joan' bedroom. "You're new here, aren't you?" asks Karen, and the scene continues, per the original script:

KAREN: *I have not been out of this house since I was brought here nine years ago. In that time, many women – young, beautiful like you – have come...I am Karen – Madame Poelzig...My father died in prison during the war. Herr Poelzig married my mother – she died when I was very young.*

JOAN: *And he married you? You are his wife?* (There is the sound of the three-tone bell downstairs, where the devil worshippers are arriving.) *What is that?*

KAREN: (hysterically) *Another bride for the Devil! Another offering to the gods of my master.* (dominating – on a crest of hysteria) *Prepare!*

The spectacle of Karen chillingly morphing from beatific angel to screaming Satan worshipper must have been a shocker! It too, was fated for a retake, but more on that later. Poelzig enters the bedroom...he picks up the cat...he follows Karen into the next room...we hear her scream...

The dark of the moon...time for the Black Mass. The disciples, meanwhile, have been arriving downstairs. The script had wanted to make more of the Satanists than we see in the release print:

... give as much as is possible the impression of complete artificiality - that they have been made of old pieces of celluloid, wire, papier-mâché, flesh and red plush by someone like Aubrey Beardsley...members, for the most part, of the decadent aristocracy of the countryside...

One grotesque the script presents – Count Windischgraetz's "dear sister Steffi," who smokes "a large, curved meerschaum pipe" ...and grunts.

The "Satanists" who answer Universal's $20 per day casting call include bald, mustached Michael Mark, father of Little Maria in *Frankenstein* and hanger-on in a number of Universal horror shows; Paul Panzer, villain of Silents and a graveside mourner in *Frankenstein*; Lois January, a Universal stock contractee; King Baggot, who'd starred in Universal's 1913 *Dr. Jekyll and Mr. Hyde*; and a tall, cadaverous 28-year old actor named John Peter Richmond - who, in 1935, would begin attracting notice under the name of John Carradine (and is fated to play the title role in Ulmer's 1944 PRC production of *Bluebeard*).

Karloff, in his $50 Ulmer-designed high priest robe, descends the great staircase, his eyes gaping; the pentagram jewelry around his neck reflecting the light... his step feline. There's a wild, bestial look in Karloff, portending that the dapper guests are fated to become orgiastic disciples as the rites of Lucifer proceed to their climax – where the high priest will rape the maiden and kill her. Inside the chapel, we see a tall, blasphemously cockeyed cross—a brazen defiance of Joseph Breen's warning. The worshippers don black robes as the organist (Carradine) eerily plays "Adagio in A Minor" from Bach's *Toccata*. Karloff's Lucifer mounts the altar, his arms swaying in ritualistic gestures, and hauntingly chants the litany of the Black Mass:

> *Cum grano salis.*
> *Fortis cadre, cedre non potest...*
> *Lupis pilum mutat non mentem.*
> *Magna est veritas, et pro evolebit...*

Along with the cockeyed cross are cockamamie Latin prayers. To translate:

> *With a grain of salt. The brave may*
> *Fall, but cannot yield.*
> *The wolf changes its skin, but not its*
>   *mind.*
> *Great is truth, and it shall prevail...*

And so it goes. The diabolists deliver Joan, clad in her white sacrificial maiden gown, to the Black Mass. Jacqueline Wells faints again. The disciples lash the virgin to the Breen Office-defying crooked cross. Poelzig turns and reaches for her...

A blonde Satanist, overcome, screams and faints. The faint suffices to distract Poelzig from his ritual rape and murder, and Werdegast moves to save the heroine.

Save her? Not in the original script and shoot! Bela's Vitus is to abscond with Joan... and try to rape her!

To Brahms' *Rhapsody in B Minor*, Vitus and Thamal take Joan into the cellars. The Majordomo shoots Thamal, who beats the Majordomo; they wound each other fatally. Joan informs Vitus that Karen, his daughter, is alive.

"She's Poelzig's wife!" she cries.

Lugosi was quiet, a little more shy, a loner. I don't recall talking to him very much. In fact, I didn't work with him in The Black Cat *except when I was "dead"! He was more aloof, and sort of stayed by himself. He was not as communicative...*

As for Bela's howl... Lucille, meanwhile, wished she could let out a howl of horror too. Frightened by Ulmer's sexual harassment, she'd told nobody of her hanging-from-her-hair torture, and now he struck again:

So...I was strapped to this operating table, with a wishbone curvature for my neck – the nape of my neck was on this iron pipe, which curved up. Ulmer fixed the pipe so tight that it cut

With directions from the dying Majordomo, Bela sees a covered corpse on a table; pulling back the sheet, he beholds his daughter, killed by her depraved husband/ stepfather. In one of his greatest all-time film moments, Bela Lugosi trembles, and lets out a magnificent howl of horror.

Oddly, both scenes Lucille played with Lugosi called for her to be a corpse – first as Karen the elder in the glass coffin, later Karen the younger on the table. In comparing Bela to Boris, she said:

off the blood supply – then, once again, he left me there while they broke for lunch.

Well, I started to bleed at the mouth. I didn't have enough sense to scream and holler, because I didn't want to make a scene. Remember Harry Cording, the great big Manchurian-looking giant, with almond-shaped eyes, who played Lugosi's bodyguard? He came back; he thought something was wrong. He saw me - and he had a fit. He got me off that table, and he took me, as I was bleeding from the mouth, and carried me to my dressing room. It was really horrendous.

677-93

They talk of "harassment" now. Well, how much more "harassed" could you be than to be left in those horrible conditions?

Poelzig, ripping off his ceremonial robes, stripped down to basic black, appears on the scene. He shoves Joan away, and Jacqueline Wells screams again. Poelzig and Werdegast fight, and the dying Thamal helps Werdegast drag his "old friend" to a rack. Jacqueline Wells, screams again. Thamal collapses and dies.

The infamous skinning alive scene of *The Black Cat* – which, of course, Ulmer was hell-bent on shooting, despite all of Joseph Breen's warnings – is one of the most haunting vignettes of all Horror Movies. Karloff, stripped to the waist, hangs on the "embalming rack" like a snared prize wolf, as Lugosi, wildly, vengefully mad, rants to his nemesis, and the "Sempre Forte ed Agitato" from Liszt's *Sonata* exhorts the overall lunacy:

Do you know what I'm going to do to you now? No? Did you ever see an animal skinned, Hjalmar? Ha, ha! That's what I am going to do to you now. Tear the skin from your body —slowly – bit by bit!

The original lines were even juicier: "I am going to tear your putrid, stinking skin from your body, Hjalmar..." Ulmer called "Action!" Bela, richly enjoying the dramatics (and, one's tempted to believe, so thrilled at skinning the top-billed, tea break-loving Boris) rips into "Did you ever see an animal *skinned*, Hjalmar?" – and garbles his English.

"Cut," called Ulmer.

"Yes, Lugosi did have trouble with that scene!" remembered Shirley Kassler Ulmer. As Dear Boris kept-a-hanging on the rack, Bela battled his emotions and the English language, and Ulmer finally gets a "take" - a *magnificent* take.

The skinning alive plays in Kafka shadow, with Jacqueline Wells unleashing yet another scream, rapidly followed by her final one in the movie. As she told me:

I had learned to scream before The Black Cat. *At first you feel so stupid* (laughing), *standing there shrieking! But it's very important to scream well. And I got so I could. I could just turn the scream on and off!*

In fact, Jacqueline became such an ace screamer that, during her 1940s sojourn at Warner Bros., where she used the stage moniker of Julie Bishop, she recorded a repertoire of screams, to be dubbed in for actresses who required help in that specialty.

The skinning alive goes on, the Liszt passages booming, a close-up of Boris's hand writhing in the manacle, and Bela ranting, "How does it feel to hang on your *own* embalming rack, Hjalmar!" To cap the sadism, Karloff lets out a feline yelp - bizarre, but totally in keeping with his brilliantly zoomorphic portrayal.

It's also the climax of Ulmer's mad religious flourishes in *The Black Cat*. For Karloff, hanging from the rack, half-naked, arms outstretched, is Lucifer Crucified – or the closest thing to it that even Edgar G. Ulmer would have dared evoke in 1934. In a wildly ironic and supremely blasphemous twist, Karloff's modern Satan chillingly becomes a Christ symbol, Lugosi's Werdegast memorably provides the scourging, and Cinema gains one its most perverse images of all time.

The revived Peter shows up as Werdegast skins Poel-zig and, locked behind a gate, calls to Joan to pry the key from the dead Thamal's hand so they can escape. Ulmer's original vision of this scene, according to the shooting script, has to be read to be believed:

An effect as if Werdegast was splitting the scalp slowly, pulling the sheath of skin over Poelzig's head and shoulders... Werdegast finishes, straightens and surveys his work with eminent satisfaction; his insane eyes turn to Joan. He starts toward her...Peter raises the Luger and fires...Werdegast staggers, falls. Joan is still trying to pry the key out of Thamal's hand in background. Poelzig, sans skin, is struggling on the rack. By a superhuman effort he frees himself and falls to the floor... Werdegast raises himself on one elbow and stares at Poelzig. He laughs hysterically, insanely...

Werdegast was to start crawling toward the dynamite switch, to blast everyone to kingdom come:

Poelzig raises his hideous body – his eyes focused dully, expressionlessly, on Joan. He laboriously, painfully crawls to her. As he comes closer, Joan, with redoubled strength, gets the key, rises and runs to the door...Poelzig with the last vestige of his strength, turns and starts crawling toward Werdegast...

What was pulpy Poelzig planning to do if he'd reached Joan? Or Werdegast? The mind boggles! At any rate, the question arises: Was this how Ulmer originally directed the scene? No stills appear to survive of a bloody, skinned-alive Karloff, eking his way along the floor - although hope springs eternal that there's one out there somewhere, proving Ulmer actually did film this remarkable grotesquerie!

In the release print, Peter, misinterpreting Werdegast's attempt to help Joan, shoots him. The honeymooners turn at the door and flee, and the dying Werdegast props himself against the wall.

It's the red switch, isn't it, Hjalmar? The red switch ignites the dynamite. Five minutes – Marmaros, you, and I, and your rotten cult – will be no more. It has been a good game," says Bela's Vitus Werdegast - a moving last line to a wonderfully intense, melancholy, and moving performance.

The dynamite sparks. As Joan and Peter escape, Ulmer had planned for them to witness an orgy among the Satanists, cavorting in the chapel and living room "in abandoned and lascivious clusters." However, Joseph Breen had decreed, "The implication of sexual intimacy in this scene should be eliminated," and there's no orgy, at least in sight.

Yet the escape of the newlyweds offers its own flourishes: Jacqueline Wells is now fetishistic. She sports one of the devil worshippers' black robes, worn as a cape, flowing behind her torn sacrificial gown, and she wears black high heels (she was barefoot in the cellars). The virgin runs, showing a Pre-Code flurry of thighs and lingerie - Edgar G. Ulmer's *Female-in-Excelsis*, evoking a gothic dominatrix Poelzig might have invited to the Black Mass. Reminded 63 years later of her kinky cape and semi-striptease, Jacqueline Wells just laughed.

"Probably, by that time, we were getting near the end - it didn't matter!"

To the rhapsody of Tchaikovsky's *Romeo and Juliet*, Fort Marmaros explodes in the night, apocalyptically. Down on the road, Peter in his torn suit and Joan with her exposed thighs easily attract headlights (in an amusing touch, Joan casually pulls her cape around her as the vehicle approaches). The script originally offers a tag in which a bus - piloted by no less than Edgar G. Ulmer, in white beard and goggles - stops.

"Will you take us to Visegrad?" asks Peter.

"I'm not going to Visegrad," replies the disguised Ulmer. "I'm going to a sanitarium to rest up after making *The Black Cat* in fourteen days! However, it will be a long walk. For you, I shall make an exception."

While this inside joke never makes the film, a comic ending does. Back on the Orient Express, a refreshed Peter and a bundled-up Joan read a newspaper review of Peter's latest mystery novel, *Triple Murder*. It claims he has fulfilled his literary promise, but overstepped credibility bounds: "These things could never by the furthest stretch of the imagination actually happen. We could wish that Mr. Alison would confine himself to the possible, instead of letting his melodramatic imagination run away with him."

Manners and Wells perform a poker-faced "take" at each other. The *Romeo and Juliet* theme swells.

THE END

A good cast is worth repeating....

CHAPTER 13

A NEAR-HEART ATTACK

....put your faith and your hope and your best on the big three in The Black Cat *– Karloff, Lugosi and Poe!*
From Universal's pressbook for *The Black Cat*

The Black Cat completes shooting Saturday, March 17, 1934 – St. Patrick's Day, and only one day over schedule.

Tuesday, March 20: "U Talking Trio with Lugosi," headlines *Variety:*

Universal is discussing three picture deal with Bela Lugosi, who just finished featured spot in "The Black Cat." Player was originally typed as a horror menace in "Dracula," although he played straight roles on the stage until leading legit vampire drama.

U untyped him in Black Cat *with a straight part, and figure he may be a good bet for that class of role.*

Meanwhile, Carl Laemmle, Sr. views the rough cut of *The Black Cat.* The result is pretty much what Laemmle, Jr. had anticipated.

"Old 'Uncle Carl' almost had a heart attack!" remembered Shirley Kassler Ulmer.

One can imagine Laemmle's outrage at son Junior, who'd sanctioned what the patriarch saw as a filmic atrocity. With pulpits denouncing Hollywood's sinful ways, *The Black Cat* seems a lightning rod for state censorship, religious condemnation, and a lambasting attack from Joe Breen. Additionally, Bela Lugosi, supposedly "untyped" and in a "straight" role, has ended up trying to rape the heroine.

Laemmle, Sr. makes it clear: Universal will *never* release this movie in its present form. Emergency action is necessary.

Sunday, March 25: The Black Cat begins three-and-a-half days of additional scenes and retakes, to make Lugosi more sympathetic, tone down the horror, and, as things evolve, add a dash of polish. A production estimate dated March 26, 1934 calls for 9,000 feet of film and a $6,500 budget.

"It drove Edgar crazy," said Shirley Kassler Ulmer, who was there for the retakes.

The company works day and night. Shot in that time:

• A new scene, following the trip to the cellars, where Werdegast stops Thamal from going to knife Poelzig. Bela's new dialogue nicely plugs many holes in the altered plot: "Not yet, Thamal. Put that away. We will bide our time. Other lives are involved, and this place is so undermined with dynamite that the slightest mistake by one of us could cause the destruction of all. Until I tell you different – you are his servant, not mine."

• New shots of the chess game, with Vitus avowing himself on the side of the angels – "I intend to let her go!" – and his ensuing close-ups of remorse when Thamal knocks out Peter.

• A milder scene between Karen and Joan, axing Karen's ravings about "another bride for the devil!"

• A benign tag for Werdegast's boudoir scene with Joan.

• New shots of Werdegast's climactic self-sacrifice in the finale.

• Process shots of the bus accident and the introductory shot of Fort Marmaros. The opening shot of the Marmaros exterior (a $175 process shot) is a glass painting by Russ Lawson, photographed by Jack Cosgrove (later the special effects photographer for *Gone With the Wind*) with rear-projected clouds. For all the Bauhaus influence, many believe Fort Marmaros owes at least some of its inspiration to the Ennis-Brown House, 2607 Glendower Avenue in the Hollywood Hills, designed by Frank Lloyd Wright, completed in the early 1920s and popularly known for years by horror buffs as "The Black Cat House."

It's also possible that Ulmer reshot several scenes in the skinning-alive episode; if filmed as scripted, it was definitely edited. Of course, for all the antiseptic-ing, the irrepressible Ulmer adds one of *The Black Cat's* most kinky episodes, gambling (correctly) that Old Man Laemmle will miss the full-blown perversion of the scene.

He's right.

It's the cellars of Fort Marmaros. The music is a strange, classical 5/4 "three-legged waltz," which Heinz Roemheld entitles *Morgue*. And the insinuation is one of the most fantastic and ghoulishly baroque of all Universal's horror shows...

To the romantic strains of *Morgue*, KARLOFF's Lucifer, lovingly stroking a black cat, haunts the Marmaros cellars, the "Room of Nightmares" in his own kinky Kingdom of Hell, slyly eyeballing the embalmed female sacrifices, preserved in vertical crystal caskets.

"The sex scene of all sex scenes!" laughed Shirley Kassler Ulmer of this fantastic perversity.

Six anonymous actresses, whose Hollywood dreams probably embraced snapping their garters for Busby Berkeley, find themselves as Poelzig's erotic corpses in this necrophilia fantasy, looking (as the *Los Angeles Times* review will claim) like "dead Follies beauties," posing in the see-through coffins and earning $12.50 each. The brazenly macabre vignette delicately suggests that these ladies had been Poelzig's brides of Satan - raped at his Black Mass altar, murdered, and by some wicked embalming magic, preserved forever for the high priest's lustful review.

"I love that scene," Shirley Ulmer told me. "Naughty, but nice!" In *Slant* Magazine, August 30, 2004, Josh Vasquez wrote:

...perhaps one of the single greatest images to come out of the Universal horror cycle is the breathtaking image of Poelzig's collection of dead women hovering in glass cases as he walks among them stroking his cat, admiring his "pussy" as it were - and meticulously designed as one of the genuine triumphs of the first period of Expressionist cinema...

Meanwhile, Universal plays down the retakes crisis, opting to tell *Variety* a story that Karloff, Lugosi, and Lionel Atwill will all star together for Universal in Robert Louis Stevenson's *The Suicide Club*. (MGM later produces it, without horror stars, as 1936's *Trouble for Two*.)

Some scenes are cut as well. Out go comic flourishes

that had preceded Werdegast's entrance, including train steward Luis Alberni, who'd played "Gecko" in John Barrymore's 1931 *Svengali*, and the train's Maître d'hôtel Herman Bing, who'd played the German who thought Erik the ape was speaking Italian in Lugosi's *Murders in the Rue Morgue*. (It is uncertain whether or not Ulmer shot the train scene in which the "large man in a gaudy dressing gown" pacing outside the train "Lavabo," and the "very attractive girl in negligee" who comes out and smiles at him.) Destined too for the cutting room floor was a comic scene in which Peter has breakfast at Marmaros, realizes the servants can't speak English, and proceeds in a voice "dripping with acid and honey," to insult the house, Poelzig, the Hungarian language, Hungary, the food, and the servants themselves who, fooled by Peter's expression, beam at his insults.

The retakes and new scenes save *The Black Cat*, and naturally fatten the wallets of most of the players. The budget sheet shows no extra money for Karloff, whose $7,500 was a "flat fee," but Lugosi picks up $583.35 for his three-and-a-half days – thereby earning a grand total of $3,583.35 and surpassing David Manners (by about $40) as the second-best paid actor in *The Black Cat*. Still, Bela earns slightly less than half of Boris's fee. As for Edgar Ulmer, he simply receives another Universal check for $150. His total pay for *The Black Cat*: $1,050.

Wednesday, March 28, 1934: Just after *The Black Cat* finishes its retakes, both Jacqueline Wells and Lucille Lund win the honor of being among the 13 WAMPAS Baby Stars of 1934. The tradition of selecting Hollywood's "cream of the crop" starlets had begun in 1922 via the Western Association of Motion Picture Advertisers, that is, WAMPAS.

Boris Karloff celebrates the passing of *The Black Cat* in a big way. The star buys a new home: a Mexican farmhouse, with pool and gardens, high in the mountains of Coldwater Canyon. The estate has three acres, and *The Hollywood Reporter* claims Boris purchases the site because the Australian Cricketers are sending him a kangaroo, and he wants room for it to play.

Saturday, March 31: *The Hollywood Reporter* announces that Heinz Roemheld, "former conductor of the Berlin Symphony Orchestra," has signed to direct the musical score for *The Black Cat*. Production reports calls for an orchestra of 28 players (as well as a one-to-six hour session for an organist). Ulmer, passionate about music, will work with Roemheld in selecting the classical pieces that will score the film.

Tuesday, April 2: The Breen Office screens a rough-cut of *The Black Cat* in the morning. Later this day, Breen writes to Universal that the film "conforms to the provisions of the Production Code and contains little, if anything, that is reasonably censorable." One wonders how carefully Breen was paying attention, as he goes on to write:

We are particularly pleased with the manner in which your studio and director have handled this subject, and we congratulate you.

Why Breen green-lights *The Black Cat*, with its cock-eyed cross and skinning-alive episode after all his warnings, is a mystery. It should be noted that Breen wrote: "For the record, you should know that three or four of the scenes were missing from the print which we saw this morning." Breen presumed they were "some kind of stock shots." Universal's Assistant General Manager Harry Zehner assured Breen that the missing footage would "not in any way violate censorship or the Code." One can only wonder!

The release date is set for May. April, meanwhile, will be full of significant happenings:

• *Tuesday, April 3:* Karloff attends the gala Hollywood premiere of *House of Rothschild* at Grauman's Chinese Theatre. Karloff's star power also jumps with the news from Broadway that *House of Rothschild*, which had premiered in New York on March 14, has set a new high at the Astor Theatre, while *The Lost Patrol*, which had opened in New York March 30, has topped records at the Rialto with a walloping $32,000 take.

• *Monday, April 9:* Aleister "The Beast" Crowley, inspiration for Hjalmar Poelzig, makes news again as he goes to court in London, suing Nina Hamnett's publisher for inferring in her book, *Laughing Torso*, that Crowley allegedly practiced human sacrifice at his Abbey of Thelema. In *Do What Thou Wilt: A Life of Aleister Crowley*, Lawrence Sutin details the trial, a disaster for "the Beast." Crowley, now "bald, stout, toothy, sallow, and eccentrically dressed, wearing an outdated top hat on his way to and from the court proceedings," grandstands in the witness box, to little effect. Perhaps the high point of the four-day trial comes when his opposing lawyer challenges Crowley to prove his magic powers, and become invisible. The Beast declines. The judge, Mr. Justice Swift, who'd been engaged in law for over 40 years, tells the jury, "I have never heard such dreadful, horrible, blasphemous and abominable stuff as that which has been produced by a man who described himself to you as the greatest living poet." Aleister Crowley not only loses, but is judged liable for the defendants' legal costs. He will pay nothing,

declaring bankruptcy in 1935.

• *Thursday, April 12:* The Hollywood Reporter notes that, "in line with its cycle of super horror pics," Universal will produce *Bluebeard* – "probably" starring Karloff, with Edgar Ulmer to direct what is planned as "an elaborate production."

• *Friday, April 13:* The Hollywood Reporter claims that Heinz Roemheld conducts a 50-player orchestra in recording the glorious score for *The Black Cat*. Once again, Uncle Carl is apoplectic, hating the idea of the classical music throughout the film; he will demand Junior rescore the entire picture. This time however, Junior will stand behind his friend Ulmer, and they win

• *Saturday, April 21:* The Hollywood Reporter announces, "U yesterday granted the request of Edgar Ulmer for a release from his contract due to difficulties over salary. Ulmer announced he would freelance."

The obvious question: What happened?

Arianne Ulmer claims the account of her father's fight for money is valid. But there's also an event worthy of nighttime soap opera: Uncle Carl discovers that Edgar and Shirley (then wed to Uncle Carl's favorite nephew Max, remember) have become romantically involved. To have a family member hurt by the man who'd made *The Black Cat* is simply too much; the almighty "Uncle Carl" banishes the "Aesthete from the Alps" from Universal City.

Before the premiere of *The Black Cat*, Edgar G. Ulmer is in exile. Blackballed, told by everyone he'll never work in movies again, he and Shirley move into the Christie Hotel in Hollywood – where, in 1932, Karloff and Lugosi had joined other foreign stars to dedicate the Christmas tree. After Shirley's divorce, she and Ulmer will marry in 1935.

All in all, *The Black Cat* had taken an official 19 days to shoot; the final revised cost sheet, dated February 16, 1935, will tally the final expense, even after the retakes, at $92,323.76. Hence, *The Black Cat* cost slightly over one-third the tab of *Frankenstein* and about one-fourth the budget for *Dracula*.

PATRICIA ELLIS CAN KICK 23 3/4 INCHES ABOVE HER HEAD!

C. HENRY GORDON HAS PLAYED ON MORE FAMOUS GOLF COURSES THAN ANY OTHER ACTOR IN HOLLYWOOD. HE HAS BEEN ALL OVER THE WORLD, AND PLAYED ALMOST DAILY.

BORIS KARLOFF WAS THE BABY OF A FAMILY OF NINE CHILDREN, AND RAN AWAY FROM HOME IN ENGLAND TO ESCAPE GOING INTO THE CONSULAR SERVICE. ELEVEN YEARS AGO HE WAS DRIVING A TRUCK IN LOS ANGELES!

SHOOTING AT THE STARS

PLAYED COUNT DRACULA IN "DRACULA" ON BOTH STAGE AND SCREEN

HEIGHT 6 FT. 1 IN. WEIGHT 179 LBS. EYES DARK BLUE HAIR DARK BROWN

ALSO PLAYED IN "MURDERS IN THE RUE MORGUE"

PLAYED IN EARL CARROLL'S STAGE PLAY "MURDER AT THE VANITIES"

FOREST AGES McGINN

Bela Lugosi

STARRING WITH KARLOFF in "BLACK CAT"

BORN IN LUGOS, HUNGARY, OCT. 29, 1884, SON OF BARON LUGOSI, A BANKER

CHAPTER 14

CAVORTING CAT

A NEW CREATURE JOINS THE KARLOFF PARADE OF MONSTERS IN *THE BLACK CAT*
BELA LUGOSI ONCE PLAYED ROMEO!
POE IS ALWAYS SUPREME
Pressbook headlines for *The Black Cat*

"BLACK CAT"

Of course, the exhibitor's pressbook, contained in this volume, accents the first teaming of Karloff and Bela Lugosi in one of Poe's "most outstanding masterpieces."

The reader can peruse these gimmicks, but just a sample:

"Giant Cat Ballyhoo": This called for two "ballyhoo men" to dress up in a giant black cat suit, emblazoned with:

Frankenstein   Dracula
KARLOFF   LUGOSI
                          In

"In walking through the streets," the pressbook suggested, "have these men cavort, leap and carry on in such a way to attract extra attention. You can be certain of stopping crowds with this stunt."

There's also a clever on-screen gimmick. As was the custom in many films of the early 1930s, the opening credits featured close-ups of the stars and featured players. For KARLOFF in *The Black Cat*, Universal selects a shot of Poelzig playing the organ and seen from the back, as if to keep the audience in suspense as to Karloff's latest cinema face. Bela Lugosi receives a traditional close-up, and a very handsome one.

Part XV

"IMPROPER FACES"

B-r-r-r-r-r! You'll see things you never WILL forget!...but you'll love it!
PR copy for *The Black Cat*

Thursday, May 3, 1934. Come a glorious blast of Liszt's *Sonata in B Minor*, and *The Black Cat* fills the screen at the Hollywood Pantages Theatre, the premiere night crowd beholding the legendary star billing:

KARLOFF
and
BELA LUGOSI

There's a special opening night treat: KARLOFF, Bela Lugosi, and Jacqueline Wells all make personal appearances. "I went with Boris and Bela to the Hollywood premiere that night," Jacqueline Wells/Julie Bishop will remember. "We were all grouped together and talked a lot. I was very excited!"

Edgar Ulmer is not at the premiere; had he been, one imagines Universal surely would have insisted that he buy his own ticket. *The Black Cat* plays the Pantages with the support of a second feature – *Cheaters*, from Poverty Row's Liberty Pictures – and a newsreel about John Dillinger. There'd been no press preview, and the morning after the big night at the Pantages, *The Hollywood Reporter* opines of *The Black Cat*:

Karloff and Bela Lugosi, the WAMPAS baby-frighteners of 1934, fight it out for seven reels for the mugging championship of the picture...Jacqueline Wells, David Manners and Lucille Lund are a trio of attractive people who surely deserve a better break...

The Hollywood Reporter sums up its review with this critique: "Karloff and Lugosi make improper faces at each other."

Friday, May 11: Universal awards Boris Karloff a new star contract, and *The Black Cat* opens at the Orpheum in San Francisco, complete with bandleader Ted Lewis, of the top hat and "Is Everybody Happy?" line, live on stage. *The San Francisco Examiner* praises *The Black Cat* as "...the most cultured horror film this department has yet witnessed," citing its classical music, "dazzlingly modernistic" sets and "expert" acting.

"Lugosi and Karloff in the pic," writes *Variety*, "plus Lewis, are a trio of good draws, and big $15,000 likely."

Also on May 11: *The Black Cat* opens at the Rialto in Washington, D.C. *The Washington Post* hails the film as a "Masterpiece of Suspense."

Boris Karloff – Bela Lugosi – Edgar Allan Poe: the perfect set-up for the very apotheosis of thrillers! And in the presentation of The Black Cat, *the goal is missed by only a very slight margin...*

The moment Bela Lugosi enters upon the scene, something is expected – something probably terrible, even horrible, yet at the same time uncannily fascinating...

Karloff, appearing as a cadaverous blend of the Frankensteinian Monster and the Mummy, is a great architect gone mad on the subject of devil worship. Lugosi, playing a "straight" role, is a psychiatrist who returns to wreak vengeance on Mr. Karloff...

...a beautiful study is The Black Cat *- that is, beautiful in construction, development and camera treatment, even though the fundamental thesis be none too savory...*

By the followers of such pictures as Frankenstein, The Mummy, White Zombie, Dracula *and others of like fabrication,* The Black Cat *will be wholeheartedly welcomed. But – if you cannot stand suspense (the sort that lingers for about an hour after the close of the picture), our advice is to take your feline vicariously!*

"Horror stuff is this spot's one sure-fire type," writes *Variety* of D.C's Rialto. "Karloff-Lugosi combo should get nice $6,000." The previous week's *Uncertain Lady* had "got by" with a "satisfactory" $3,000.

Thursday, May 17: *The Black Cat* plays a preview tonight at Broadway's Roxy Theatre.

Friday, May 18: "IT'S TREMONSTROUS!" hails the Universal publicity as *The Black Cat* has its official Broadway premiere at the Roxy Theatre, complete with a "Gala New Stage Show," featuring several acrobatic troupes and the Gae Foster Girls. The weather is appropriate: there are two thunderstorms in New York that weekend, as well as hail. Meanwhile, this weekend in L.A., Boris and Bela are among the many Hollywood stars appearing in person at the Screen Actors Guild "Film Stars Frolic." They even guest-star together in a short subject on the "Frolic", Columbia's *Screen Snapshots # 11*.

The big attractions at the time on the Great White Way: Joan Crawford in MGM's *Sadie McKee* at the Capitol, Irene Dunne in RKO's *Stingaree* at Radio City Music Hall, Shirley Temple in Paramount's *Little Miss Marker* at the Paramount, and *House of Rothschild* in its 10th week at the Astor.

Tuesday, May 22: Variety, "the show business Bible," pans *The Black Cat*:

Because of the presence in one film of Boris Karloff, that jovial madman, and Bela Lugosi, that suave fiend, this picture probably has box office attraction. But otherwise and on the counts of story, novelty, thrills and distinction, it is sub-normal...

The trade paper lambasts the skinning-alive vignette ("A truly horrible and nauseating bit of extreme sadism ...dubious showmanship"), as well as the Black Mass ("also close to the border"). "Karloff and Lugosi are sufficiently sinister and convincingly demented," writes the reviewer. "Jacqueline Wells spends most of her footage in swoons." *Variety's* most colorful prose devoted to *The Black Cat*: "Clash of the two eyebrow-squinting nuts."

Also on Tuesday, May 22: "Overboard on Cats," headlines *Variety*, citing this PR debacle in Indianapolis:

Duke Hickey, advance man for Universal, became inspired with the idea of holding a special showing of The Black Cat at the Lyric on Saturday morning and allowing every child under sixteen accompanied by a solid black cat, free admission to the theatre. House staff was driven nearly frantic with nearly a hundred badly frightened felines who objected with all claws to being legal tender for their masters' admission to the picture. Unused office on mezzanine floor was finally drafted into service as an emergency jail for the cats until end of screening. A new problem arose when owners tried to identify their own particular solid black cat. Performance was enjoyed mostly by members of house staff who had no hand in caring for the animals.

Meanwhile, as to box office...*Variety* reports *The Black Cat's* one-week engagement tally at the Roxy at $22,000. This was in a theatre where the recent high had been Universal's *The Invisible Man* ($42,000), the recent low Columbia's *Air Hostess* ($9,000). The figure placed *The Black Cat* just below the median for the Roxy. It was, however, the Roxy's best take in several weeks; the previous week's film, Universal's *Glamour*, starring Junior Laemmle's heartthrob Constance Cummings, had taken in $17,000.

Monday, May 28: "Cinema's two outstanding blood-curdlers deserve a better vehicle than *The Black Cat* in which to appear together for the first time," critiques *Time* magazine. It labels the film "A dismal hocus-pocus" and describes the climax thusly:

...with that grisly bout of Satanism, they swing into action, shrieking, shooting, skulking, fainting, sprinting, cursing and puffing...Silly shot: the Black Mass, with Karloff intoning Latin gibberish.

Meanwhile a new problem arises: Censorship.

At the time of *The Black Cat's* release, the Breen Office is about to become far more vigilant, as is the Roman Catholic Church's Legion of Decency, founded in 1933. The Legion had created the "Condemned" rating, applying it to such films as MGM's *Queen Christina* (in which Greta Garbo dressed as a man) and *Men in White* (in which Elizabeth Allan underwent an abortion). Somehow *The Black Cat* eludes the Condemned rating, but in Chicago, the Rev. F. G. Deenan of the Society of Jesus puts together his own list, rating *The Black Cat* as a "Class B" attraction - "Pictures in this group may be considered offensive because they are suggestive in spots, vulgar, sophisticated or lacking in modesty." Actually, in "Class B," *The Black Cat* enjoys distinguished company - including *Little Miss Marker* and the movie that will win the 1934 Best Picture Academy Award, *It Happened One Night!*

Meanwhile, there are censors in the various states and "territories." Even before *The Black Cat* had shot a frame of film, Joseph Breen had warned of its possible "mutilation" by the local boards. Among the mutilators:

• Maryland eliminates "All references to flaying victim alive, and silhouette of doctor using knife."

• Ohio axes Bela's "Did you ever see an animal skinned..." speech, the shot of him selecting a knife, and all scenes of the skinning – as well as "scene of Poelzig's hand fastened in metal handcuff, twisting and turning." Chicago cut most of this as well.

• Ontario performs multiple excisions, including the cat's scream after Werdegast throws a knife at it, the name of the narcotic "Hyoscine," and, in final reel 7, makes *12* trims and cuts – including Joan tied to the cross, Werdegast "fastening man to cross (*sic*) and stripping man's clothes off," Bela's "Did you ever..." lines, and all scenes with "view of man skinning man alive with accompanying screams and dialogue."

Monday, June 4: Boris Karloff is a guest star tonight on radio's *The Show,* performing a scene from *Dr. Jekyll and Mr. Hyde.*

Tuesday, June 5: Jimmy Starr, who'd so merrily fanned the fire of a Karloff/Lugosi animosity, reports in his column:

The Bela (Dracula) Lugosi and Boris (Frankenstein) Karloff FEUD can continue, along its "I'll-sneer-at-you" way. Bela's been signed to a term contract at Universal.

Monday, June 25: Amidst the "mutilation," *Variety* runs a headline: "Catholic Women Put Oke On 13 for Church Shows." Although Fr. Deenan labeled *The Black Cat* a "Class B" attraction, the Motion Picture Bureau of the International Foundation of Catholic Alumnae, eager to endorse films as well as condemn them, has put together a list of 13 recently released films, "suitable for family night programs" and "recommended for showing in Church halls and Catholic Schools." In the list: *The Black Cat -* rated by the ladies as "Very Good"!

Internationally, the film faces far less tolerance.

• Australia cuts the shadow shot of the skinning and demands all publicity bear the warning, <u>SUITABLE ONLY FOR ADULTS</u>.

• Quebec also scissors the skinning alive.

• The United Kingdom, where *The Black Cat* receives the new title of *The House of Doom,* is totally aghast – cutting Boris and Lucille in bed, lines referring to devil worship, the mummified beauties Ulmer had added in the retakes, the glimpse of Poelzig's book *Rites of Lucifer* ("and all references to same in dialogue") and the Black Mass (the inference in England is that Poelzig is into "sun worship"). The U.K. apparently retains the skinning.

• Poland cuts "The ceremony and worship of the cult of Evil and all scenes with the cross." Reason given: "These scenes are profaning the Christian religion."

• Sweden removes the shot of Thamal knocking Peter to the floor, the scene of Werdegast in Joan's room (no reason given), the Majordomo and maid on the balcony (again, no reason given), the scene of the shooting and fight between Thamal and the Majordomo, as well as the "fight between Werdegast and Poelzig and the entire ritual ceremony, also the scourging."

• Japan makes curious cuts, including this scene, which the censor describes quite nicely: "Eliminate scene of Dr .(sic) Poelzig grasping an ornament found on the table as though to try to steady the passion boiling within himself which was caused by seeing Peter and his wife passionately kissing." Also Japan cuts Poelzig and Karen in bed together; "the last and longest" of three kisses Peter and Joan shared in the boudoir; Karen's dialogue, "Oh no, you are mistaken. My father died in prison. Herr Poelzig married my mother. She died when I was very young"; and the close-up of Thalmal "with the blood running down from the corner of his mouth." The Japanese censor makes no cuts in the Black Mass and skinning alive scenes.

• Edgar Ulmer's native Austria bans *The Black Cat* outright ("Because religious feelings are hurt by the broad showing of the devil services and by the fact that one main figure, an Austrian, is shown as [a] military traitor and main criminal, thus offending the national feeling of the people"). Finland, Malaya, and Italy also ban the film. That last country, Italy, which has the distinction of having exiled Aleister Crowley, perhaps best sums up its rejection of *The Black Cat:* "Because it may create horror."

Yet a wild and wicked cinema black magic prevails. The awesome billing of "KARLOFF and BELA LU-GOSI" and the almost overpowering alchemy of the two stars, triumph over a vicious press, international censorship, the contempt of the president of the very studio that had produced the film, and the uneasy relationship of Boris and Bela. Although filmed so cheaply that it almost has to make money, the final tally is nevertheless impressive: *The Black Cat* will be Universal's hit of the season. The domestic rental is $242,000; the foreign rental $196,000; the world-wide rental, $438,000.

The profit: a very respectable $155,000.

677-P68

Karloff and Lucille Lund, in bed together in this Pre-Code shot in what Ms. Lund called "the Glamour Boudoir." The sheet above covers the one-piece fishnet lingerie that Ulmer had designed for Lucille to wear.

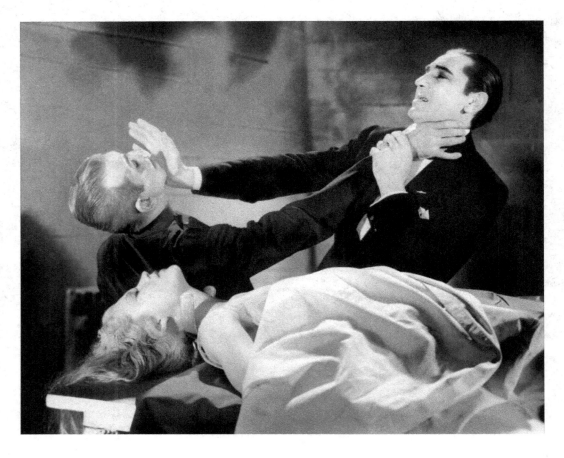

CHAPTER 16

POSTERITY

Karloff and Lugosi, despite their very different acting styles, both devour the screen.... Seeing them go head-to-head is a great treat.

Jeffrey Anderson, in his *Combustible Celluloid* DVD review of *The Black Cat* (November 2, 2005).

At five o'clock in the morning of October 7, 1849, Edgar Allan Poe, wracked by alcohol, roused himself in Washington College Hospital in Baltimore, cried out "God help my poor soul!" and died. Many believe he would have reacted the same way if he had somehow lived to see *The Black Cat*.

True, Poe's tale of revenge suggests itself in the film only via Poelzig's black cat pet. Nevertheless, Poe actually might have found much to admire, for few films have ever evoked the twisted Evil that haunted Poe's tales as did *The Black Cat*. Surely the nightmarish motifs of revenge, souls that have been "killed," and all that demonic flamboyance would have fascinated Poe - as would have the marriage of Poelzig and stepdaughter Karen. After all, Poe had married his beloved Virginia (who was truly the "core and meaning" of his life, and whose death nearly destroyed him) when she was only 13 years old. As Philip Van Doren Stern noted in his introduction to *The Portable Poe*, Poe's personality indicated "he was sexually abnormal, but there is no way of proving it."

80 years after its wildly troubled shoot, *The Black Cat* is most amazing in its striking exotica - a midnight sex and horror show, starring KARLOFF as Satan himself. That the usually demonic BELA LUGOSI is the hero only adds to the film's remarkably subversive aura. Of all the Universal horror classics, *The Black Cat* surely takes the prize for the perverse - from Jacqueline Wells's "hyper-virginal" bride to Lucille Lund's sexed-up Rapunzel, from the flashes of the heroine's thighs to the full-length female corpses in the crystal coffins - yes, even in the sly way Karloff strokes his cat! The film deliriously delivers, right up to its mad climax: Boris's modern Lucifer, hanging half-naked on a rack, virtually crucified, skinned alive by the beaming Bela. And all the while, the auburn-haired virgin watches in her torn sacrificial robe, beholding the horror more in fascination than fear - and unleashing her loudest scream.

The Black Cat is a wonderful showcase for the "im-proper faces" of Karloff and Lugosi, their powerhouse performances and macabre chemistry making their union vital cinema history. Edgar Ulmer's story, sets, costumes and brilliance had created the ideal Bauhaus backdrop for the spectacle. Karloff's Lascivious Lucifer vs. Lugosi's Avenging Angel transcend the horror movie genre, and *The Black Cat* spits, purrs, and howls its way to become a grand, lunatic fairy tale - sparked by a wickedly imaginative director, a bewitched camera, a properly epic classical score, and the most glorious teaming of horror cinema's two superstars.

What do I see of my father in The Black Cat? *Well, first of all, the Bauhaus influence. When Karloff's stroking the lady bronze piece, our house had elements of this - bronze statues and such that were part of our everyday living. Of course, the music is very much a part of my father. There's the deliberate modulation of Bela Lugosi's voice, which in some ways is very similar to my father's extremely deep voice and heavy, thick accent. And my father, with his great eyes and incredible voice, had an erotic quality about him - as does the film. When I see* The Black Cat, *it's chemically right, it's familiar - like I'm in the presence of people who are my own skin!*

Arianne Ulmer, interview with the author, 2001

Carl Laemmle, Sr. lost Universal City in March of 1936 to new management. Nevertheless, his blackballing power remained monolithic; Edgar G. Ulmer, exiled from Hollywood by Uncle Carl, labored in the east, directing such films as the Yiddish production *The Singing Blacksmith* (1938) and the black cast *Moon Over Harlem* (1939). Only after Laemmle, Sr.'s death on September 24, 1939, did Ulmer eventually gain a tenuous grasp on Hollywood.

He began his (in)famous work at Producers Releasing Corporation during World War II, creating such striking movies as *Bluebeard* (1944, starring John Carradine in the title role) and *Detour* (1945, with Ann Savage as Vera, the terrifying *femme fatale*). The miniscule budgets and six-day shooting schedule are stuff of legend- *Bluebeard*, for example, had a final cost of $167,567.42 and took 19 days to shoot - but Ulmer still frequently worked miracles as he transcended limitations.

Why Ulmer behaved the way he did on *The Black Cat*, tormenting Lucille Lund, is a mystery. Was he a disturbed man? Did he think the director of *The Black Cat* should *act* like a disturbed man? Whatever the psyche, his wife Shirley stayed loyal and devoted, personally and professionally, assisting him in all of his films over the next thirty years.

"We worked day and night," said Shirley. "You didn't get to eat or sleep - you just had to be crazy!"

The 1950s found Ulmer crafting such films as *The Man from Planet X* (1951) and *Daughter of Dr. Jekyll* (1957). His movies became family affairs. Arianne (who later attended the Royal Academy of Dramatic Arts) played in several Ulmer films as a child, and she later acted for him as the villainous "Markova" in *Beyond the Time Barrier*. *(1960)* (She even starred in the 1959 nudist movie, *Naked Venus*, that Ulmer directed under the name of Gaston Hakim). He became a cult figure and, to the end of his life, he was a passionately creative man. Shirley Ulmer movingly told me:

My poor, dear Edgar – he had three strokes. He was so terribly ill, I almost prayed that God would take him. But, as ill as he was, he still had the brain. At the very end, all he could move was the forefinger of his right hand; but I would bring him an ink pad and put the pen in his hand, and he would write his thoughts. I still have them.

Edgar George Ulmer died at the Motion Picture Country House on September 30, 1972. He was 68 years old.

As for Junior Laemmle, who unleashed Edgar Ulmer to create *The Black Cat* -he went on to produce personally such Universal classics as *Bride of Frankenstein* (1935) and *Show Boat* (1936), but after the studio's sale in 1936, he never produced another picture. He became ill, suffered from multiple sclerosis, never married, and died at his home, 1641 Tower Grove Drive above Beverly Hills, on September 24, 1979, at the age of 71.

His death came on the 40th anniversary of the death of Carl Laemmle, Sr.

As for other significant personalities from *The Black Cat*...Aleister Crowley faded into obscurity after his 1934 trial. Come the end of his life, he was living in a boarding house in Hastings, England. "These long, lonely evenings," lamented "The Beast." "They are so boring..." Crowley died December 1, 1947; his ashes were sent to his followers in America.

Nina Hamnett, whose memoir *Laughing Torso* had inspired Crowley's disastrous law suit, became known as London's "Queen of Bohemia." She died December 16, 1956, at age 66, having jumped or fallen from her apartment window and been impaled on a fence forty feet below.

The Black Cat was the final horror film for David Manners. He penned novels, joined friends in developing a guest ranch in the California desert, and spent much of his final years writing on spiritual topics. In the late 1970s, after many years in the Pacific Palisades, Manners moved to Santa Barbara and, after the death of his companion, writer William Mercer, eventually entered a nursing home there. He continued his interest in the metaphysical, trying to elude those who pursued him for stories of Old Hollywood. (Sir Ian McKellen got a story or two about James Whale from Manners during the shooting of *Gods and Monsters*). On the evening of December 23, 1998, David Manners sat in his wheelchair at the dinner table in his nursing home in Santa Barbara, stopped eating, and peacefully died. The actor was a venerable 98 years old.

As for *The Black Cat's* two leading ladies...

Julie Bishop, the screaming-and-fainting Joan, died August 30, 2001, her 87th birthday. Highlights of her Warner Bros. stardom were as leading lady to Humphrey Bogart in *Action in the North Atlantic* and Errol Flynn in *Northern Pursuit*, both in 1943. Later films included *Sands of Iwo Jima* (1949) and *The High and the Mighty* (1954), both with John Wayne. She also starred in the 1952/1953 TV series *My Hero*, with Robert Cummings. Her final film: *The Big Land* (1957). A remarkable lady who flew her own plane even in her 80s, Julie was the mother of actress Pamela Shoop (whose many credits include the role of "Nurse Karen" in 1981's *Halloween II*), headed various charities, and lived her final years with her husband, former Beverly Hills plastic surgeon Dr. William Bergin, in a cliffside house in Mendocino, California. As she spoke to me on the telephone in the spring of 1997, Julie was so fascinated that *The Black Cat* had a cult audience, and so flattered by my interest in her and the film, that she made a remarkable offer - she promised to contact a photographer and pose with her own black cat, Tiffany.

"I have a black cat now - Tiffany, called Tiffy," Julie told me. "...She has bright yellow eyes and this huge black tail. And she gets these weird expressions on her face - if they were making *The Black Cat* today, she'd be ideal for

David Manners, late in life.

Jacqueline Wells, in negligee and with her cat Tiffany, 1997.

Lucille Lund, 1993.

the part. She is gorgeous!"

Shortly afterwards a package arrived in the mail - two color 8 x 10s of Julie with Tiffany. And Julie had allowed herself to get so into the spirit of *The Black Cat* that, for one of the shots, the 82-year old, still attractive actress posed in a full black negligee.

High Priest Poelzig and Dr. Werdegast would surely have made "improper faces."

As for Lucille Lund, *The Black Cat's* hapless Karen and her cadaver mother, she passed away in Palos Verdes, California, February 16, 2002, at the age of 89. Although she'd retired in the late 1930s following shorts with The Three Stooges and Charley Chase, this beautiful lady made a "comeback" in the 1990s as a guest at film conventions. (She even appeared onstage in Los Angeles in an interview with Arianne Ulmer at a revival of *The Black Cat*.) In 1995, at the FANEX convention in Baltimore, I had the honor of presenting Lucille with her FANEX award plaque. Lucille made a gracious speech, delighting the audience and ending with a reference to her "glamour boudoir scene" of *The Black Cat*:

"I really think the reason you all remember me," said Lucille Lund, "is because I went to bed with Boris Karloff!"

Bela was a kind and lovable man, and I remember our work together with affection.

Boris Karloff

On July 2, 1934, Universal began filming *Gift of Gab*, a comedy/drama about radio. Edmund Lowe and Gloria Stuart starred, and KARLOFF and BELA LUGOSI made cameo appearances with other Universal stars - Roger Pryor, Chester Morris, Binnie Barnes, Paul Lukas, and June Knight - in a murder mystery skit.

The two stars would act together in six more films: *The Raven* (1935); *The Invisible Ray* (1936); *Son of Frankenstein* (1939); and *Black Friday* (1940), all produced by Universal; and *You'll Find Out* (1940) and *The Body Snatcher* (1945), both produced by RKO. They also worked together on radio and in personal appearances.

Their story is a moving Hollywood saga: Lugosi dying August 16, 1956, age 73, a recovering drug addict, cruelly humbled, buried in his Dracula cape; Karloff dying February 2, 1969, age 81, a millionaire living legend. Their personal relationship is too complex to cover here,

but perhaps one story will serve for now.

Tatiana Ward is a British actress who has an unusual connection to the Two Horror Superstars: her uncles had come from Hungary, and knew and loved their fellow émigré Bela Lugosi; and, as a child in the 1960s, Tatiana lived in Cadogan Square in London, where her neighbor was Boris Karloff. Lugosi had died before she was born, and she was aware that Mr. Karloff, "a fine old-fashioned gentleman" with "beautiful wise old eyes" and "that wonderful voice," had acted with Lugosi in Hollywood.

As Ms. Ward tells the story:

On one occasion I was given a picture by an older cousin, a still from Dracula, *which for some reason frightened me. It was of the Count, peering out from a tree... "Dracula," unsmiling and in shadows; Lugosi looking the true boyar, darkly magnificent as he glares out at the viewer.*

It was those glaring, angry eyes and that cloaked figure surrounded by shadows that so frightened me as a little girl and was so at odds with the photos in our albums featuring the various Hungarian get-togethers with Bela and the other Old Country men, jackets off, ties askew, everyone a bit overweight with their arms draped around one another, swearing eternal friendship and looking worse for wear. It looked like two different people, very confusing to a small child, and being so young I could not make the connection between that dark picture and the nice Mr. Lugosi that my home took such pride in. So I took the picture to show Mr. Karloff...

Boris sat with me, looking at the picture, and told me what a lovely man Bela was, and how he deeply loved children.

I piped up, "Mr. Lugosi is in Heaven."

And Mr. Karloff said, "Yes, love, that's right."

The End

THE BLACK CAT

Studio: Universal
Producer: Carl Laemmle, Jr.
Director: Edgar G. Ulmer
Supervisor: E.M. Asher
Screenplay: Peter Ruric (from a story by Ulmer and Ruric, suggested by the 1843 tale "The Black Cat" by Edgar Allan Poe)
Art Director: Charles D. Hall (Edgar G. Ulmer, uncredited)
Cinematographer: John J. Mescall
Musical Director: Heinz Roemheld
Film Editor: Ray Curtiss
Makeup Artist: Jack P. Pierce
Special Effects: John P. Fulton, Jack Cosgrove, David Horsley, Russell Lawson
Costumes: Vera West, Ed Ware (Edgar G. Ulmer, uncredited)
Assistant Directors: W.J. Reiter, Sam Weisenthal
2nd Cameraman: King Gray
Assistant Cameraman: John Martin
Script Clerk: Moree Herring
Assistant Script Clerk: Shirley Kassel
Supervisor's Secretary: Peggy Vaughn
Running Time: 65 minutes

Produced at Universal City, California, 28 February – 17 March, 1934; additional scenes and retakes, 25 March -27 March, 1934.

Los Angeles Premiere: Pantages Theatre, Hollywood, 3 May 1934.
New York City Premiere: Roxy Theatre, 18 May 1934.

The Players

Hjalmar Poelzig..KARLOFF
Dr. Vitus Werdegast........................BELA LUGOSI
Peter Alison..David Manners
Joan Alison.....Jacqueline Wells (aka Julie Bishop)
Karen...Lucille Lund
Majordomo...Egon Brecher
Thamal...Harry Cording
The Sergeant..................................Henry Armetta
The Lieutenant.................................Albert Conti
TheMaid...Anna Duncan

Train Conductor..............................Andre Cheron
Car Steward...Herman Bing
Train Steward.....................................Luis Alberni
Bus Driver..George Davis
A Porter...Alphonse Martell
A Policeman...Tony Marlow
Stationmaster...Paul Weigel
A Waiter...Albert Polet
A Brakeman.............................Rodney Hildebrand
DevilWorshippers.....................Virginia Ainsworth, King Baggot, Symona Boniface, John George, Lois January, Michael Mark, Paul Panzer, John Peter Richmond (aka John Carradine), Peggy Terry, Harry Walker

ADDENDA

1.   Other script drafts that preceded Edgar Ulmer's and Peter Ruric's *The Black Cat* included 1932's *The Brain Never Dies*, that combined Poe's *The Fall of the House of Usher* with the saga of a cat with a half a human brain. Stanley Bergerman (Junior Laemmle's brother-in-law, who produced *The Mummy*) and Jack Cunningham were the authors. There was also 1933's *The Black Cat* script, a tale of wicked Count Brandos, who entraps a young couple in his Carpathian castle and tries to drive the cat-fearing female mad with various tortures. Brandos also hopes to mate the lady with his insane son Fejos, to perpetuate his lineage. Tom Kilpatrick and Dale Van Every, who wrote this script, later collaborated on Paramount's *Dr. Cyclops* (1940).

2.   Various accounts of *The Black Cat* have Carl Laemmle, Sr. in Germany and Carl Laemmle, Jr. in New York City during the shoot. However, both *Variety* and *The Hollywood Reporter* have many articles proving both men were at Universal City throughout the entire filming.

3.   Thursday, March 1, 1934: *Variety* writes that Andy Devine, a Universal contract player, has completed his role on loan to RKO in *Stingaree* and "goes into *Black Cat* at U lot." He is, of course, nowhere to be seen in the release print. Perhaps he appeared in a "cameo" on the train...maybe as the "large man in gaudy dressing gown" who follows the "very attractive girl in negligee" after she leaves the "Lavabo"?

4.   Monday, March 12, 1934: *Variety* reported that Egon Brecher, the Majordomo of *The Black Cat*, and his wife had hosted "a Vienna supper" at their home the previous night in honor of Eva Le Gallienne, Brecher's director and leading lady in her recently-disbanded Civic

Repertory Theatre. Among the 150 persons present: Paul Muni, Josephine Hutchinson, Joseph Schildkraut, Jean Muir, Douglass Dumbrille, and *The Black Cat's* Edgar Ulmer and David Manners. *Variety* noted that, at the supper, "Carlos Hayes, composer, played his new operetta overture, *The Magic Voice*, on the piano. "

5.   Peter Ruric, after *The Black Cat*, contributed to only a handful of films (one of which was RKO's 1944 *Mademoiselle Fifi*, produced by Val Lewton, prime mover of such horror classics as 1945's *The Body Snatcher*). In *Midnight Marquee's Actor Series: Boris Karloff*, Dennis Fischer writes that Ruric's cigarette girl wife Virginia (whom Ruric had convinced to change her name to "Mushel") jumped out a window of the couple's third story Hollywood apartment in March, 1940, after "a drunken quarrel with her husband." She only injured her arm. "Mushel" remembered that Bela Lugosi visited them, perhaps grateful that Ruric had provided him so fine a role in *The Black Cat*. Ruric and Mushel divorced in 1943, and he reportedly remarried, pursuing work in Spain and North Africa ("both havens," wrote Fischer, "for penniless writers"). Ruric's final stab at success as a TV writer failed, and he died of cancer in North Hollywood, California, June 23, 1966, at the age of 64.

6.   In addition to his virtuoso work on Edgar Ulmer's *The Black Cat* and James Whale's *Bride of Frankenstein*, John J. Mescall was cinematographer on Universal's *Show Boat* (1936) and *The Road Back* (1937), both directed by Whale. Mescall received an Academy nomination for his camerawork on Paramount's *Take a Letter, Darling* (1942), directed by Mitchell Leisen. His career suffered due to his alcoholism, and his final feature was Roger Corman's *Not of This Earth* (1957). At least one account of Mescall's later life claims he ended up on Los Angeles' Skid Row. John J. Mescall died in Los Angeles County February 10, 1962, at the age of 63.

7.   Harry Cording, who played Thamal, was born in England April 26, 1891. In addition to acting in many Universal horror films - *Tower of London* (1939), *The Ghost of Frankenstein* (1942), *The Mummy's Tomb* (1942), and more - he appeared in eight of the Basil Rathbone/Nigel Bruce *Sherlock Holmes* films, starting with 20th Century-Fox's *The Adventures of Sherlock Holmes*, and then carrying on in seven of the Universal entries. He also played in such major films as *The Adventures of Robin Hood* (Warner Bros., 1938) and *For Whom the Bell Tolls* (Paramount, 1943). In the early 1950s he appeared in episodes of several early TV westerns, including *The Lone Ranger* , *Hopalong Cassidy*, and *Adventures of Wild Bill Hickok*. Harry Cording died in Sun Valley, California on September 1, 1954, at the age of 63.

8.   Egon Brecher , who played the Majordomo, was born in the same city as Edgar Ulmer - Olmutz, in what is now the Czech Republic - on February 16, 1880. He was director of Vienna's Stadts Theatre , emigrated to America in 1921, and became the acclaimed character star of Eva Le Gallienne's Civic Repertory Theatre, playing the title roles in Ibsen's *John Gabriel Borkman* and *The Master Builder*. His later films included *Mark of the Vampire* (with Lugosi, MGM, 1935), *WereWolf of London* (Universal, 1935, as the priest), *The Black Room* (with Karloff, Columbia, 1935), *Devil's Island* (with Karloff, Warner Bros., 1938), *Manpower* (Warner Bros., 1941), *Hitler's Children* (RKO, 1943), and *The Wife of Monte Cristo* (PRC, 1946, directed by Edgar Ulmer). Egon Brecher died in Hollywood on August 12, 1946, at the age of 66.

9.   In *Edgar G. Ulmer: A Filmmaker at the Margins*, Noah Isenberg writes that, "in the immediate months after *The Black Cat*," Ulmer directed "a deeply impoverished, long-forgotten B western" entitled *Thunder Over Texas*. Max Alexander produced for his "Beacon Productions," and Shirley Kassel Alexander (then still technically wed to Alexander, but having left him for Ulmer) wrote the script. Considering the tempestuous marriage break-up during *The Black Cat*, the collaboration of Ulmer, Alexander, and Shirley on this woebegone 1934 western is, to say the least, surprising. Also surprising is that Ulmer directed *Thunder Over Texas* under the name of "John Warner" - his first wife's name was Joen Warner!

10.   *The Black Cat's* re-release title in 1951 was *The Vanishing Body*.

11.   *The Black Cat* was part and parcel of the original *Shock! Theatre* package, which became a TV sensation in the fall of 1957. At the time, all of the film's major talents were still alive, except for Bela Lugosi.

12.   Hammer's *Kiss of the Vampire* (1962) strikes many as an unofficial remake of *The Black Cat*.

13.   In October, 1962, Boris Karloff was starring with Vincent Price and Peter Lorre in American-International Pictures' *The Raven*. Columnist Bob Thomas visited the set to interview the trio, and mentioned to Karloff how sad it as that Lugosi had "died broke." In his response, Karloff, usually the discreet gentleman, sounded a bit exasperated: "Yes, but that was Bela's own fault. He refused to learn the language. Once when we were doing a picture together, he asked me to help him with some lines. I learned to my horror that he was saying his lines almost phonetically. He even surrounded himself with

people who couldn't speak good English. He never learned, so he limited his own career."

14. Clips from *The Black Cat* appear in Columbia's 1968 film, *Head*, starring The Monkees. The film also offers footage from such films as *Gilda* (Columbia, 1946), as well as shots of the Rockettes. Jack Nicholson was one of the film's writers. *Head* is also the final feature credit of Tor Johnson, bald, massive wrestler/actor, memorable in the Ed Wood films.

15. Shirley Ulmer continued working, a script supervisor on such TV shows as *S.W.A.T.* (1975) and *CHIPS* (1977); she also wrote a book, *The Role of Script Supervision in Film and Television*. Devoted to the end to the memory and legacy of her complex spouse, she died July 6, 2000 in Los Angeles, at the age of 86, and is buried with her husband in the New Beth Olam Mausoleum at Hollywood Forever Cemetery.

16. Arianne Ulmer has been very involved in directing dubbing work (she herself was the Italian voice for Elke Sommer and Jean Seberg), film marketing, and her own company, AUC Films. Arianne heads the Edgar G. Ulmer Preservation Corp., "committed to the preservation and propagation of the work of independent pioneering filmmakers."

17. There are many other film versions of *The Black Cat*. To mention only two: Universal's *The Black Cat* (1941), directed by Albert S. Rogell, starred Basil Rathbone, Hugh "Woo-Woo" Herbert, Broderick Crawford, Bela Lugosi (as a scruffy caretaker) and Gale Sondergaard; the horror/comedy had no relation to Poe's tale, nor the 1934 film. American International's *Tales of Terror* (1962), a trilogy of Poe tales directed by Roger Corman, features *The Black Cat* as its middle segment, mixed with Poe's tale "The Cask of Amontillado." Peter Lorre's "Montresor" walls up his wife "Annabel" (Joyce Jameson) and her lover "Fortunato" (Vincent Price). It, too, is played largely for laughs.

18. On April 13, 2009, a jury convicted producer/songwriter Phil Spector of having killed model and actress Lana Clarkson in his Los Angeles mansion on the night of February 3, 2003, having shot her in the mouth. In the sensationalism of the trial, word spread that Spector, during a previous marriage to Ronnie Spector (lead singer of "The Ronettes"), had kept a glass coffin in his basement and had warned Ronnie to stay faithful to him, or she'd end up dead in the glass coffin, "like Snow White." The story evokes Poelzig's female cadavers on display in crystal caskets in *The Black Cat.*

19. Film historian Tom Weaver saw a revival *The Black Cat* in recent years at the Film Forum in New York City. He recalls there was "not a peep from the audience during the last fifteen minutes!"

20. On November 7, 2009, Heritage Auction Galleries in Dallas Texas auctioned Karloff's costume from *The Black Cat* – the black shirt and slacks he wears under his robe in the "Glamour Boudoir" scene with Lucille Lund, and under his high priest robes in the climax of the film. Both shirt and slacks had a United Costumers tag, each with Karloff's name handwritten in black ink. The starting bid was $10,000, the estimate $20,000, and the final realized price soared to over $90,000.

21. Lillian Lugosi Donlevy was the widow of actor Brian Donlevy, whom she wed in 1966, and who died in 1972. Lillian died in 1981.

Research Sources

As documented below, the author's research on *The Black Cat* goes back 40 years. Most sincere thanks to all the following:

Interviews

Arianne Ulmer Cipes: Telephone interview, Sherman Oaks, CA, 13 September 2001.

Lillian Lugosi Donlevy: Telephone interview, Culver City, CA, 13 December, 1974; In-person interview, Culver City, CA, 31 July 1976.

Jewel Firestine: Telephone Interview, Fort Worth, TX, 28 October 1993.

Hope Lugosi: Telephone interviews, Honolulu, HI, 15 July 1993; 12 August 1993; 19 November 1994.

Lucille Lund: Telephone interview, Malibu, CA, 19 November 1991; In-person interviews, Malibu, CA, 17, July 1992 and 31,July 1998.

David Manners: In-person interview, Pacific Palisades, CA, 30 July 1976.

Bernice Firestine McGee: Telephone interview, Fort Worth, TX, 28 October 1993.

Shirley Ulmer: Telephone interviews, Los Angeles, 8 March 1988, and 24 March 1988

Jacqueline Wells: Telephone interview, Mendocino, CA, 3 April 1997.

Actors Series: Boris Karloff (Midnight Marquee Press, Baltimore, 1995 and 1996)

Archival Collections

Billy Rose Library for the Performing Arts, Lincoln Center, New York City

National Film Information Service, Margaret Herrick Library, Academy of Motion Picture Arts and Sciences – Thanks to Ms. Kristine Krueger, NFIS coordinator

Screen Actors Guild Archives – Thanks to Valerie Yaros, Curator

University of Southern California Library, Performing Arts Collection – Thanks to Ned Comstock, curator

Books

Bojarski, Richard, *The Films of Bela Lugosi* (Citadel Press, Secaucus, NJ, 1980) and *The Films of Boris Karloff* (Citadel Press, Secaucus, NJ, 1974)

Brunas, John, Michael Brunas and Tom Weaver, *Universal Horrors, The Studio's Classic Films, 1931 – 1946,* 2nd Edition (McFarland and Co., Publishers, Jefferson, NC, 2007)

Curtis James, *James Whale: A New World of Gods and Monsters* (Faber & Faber, London, 1998)

Isenberg, Noah, *Edgar G. Ulmer: A Filmmaker at the Margins* (University of California Press, 2014)

Lindsay, Cynthia, *Dear Boris* (Alfred A. Knopf, New York 1975)

McCarthy, Todd and Charles Flynn, *Kings of the Bs* (E.P. Dutton, New York, 1975)

Rhodes, Gary Don, *Lugosi: His Life in Films, on Stage, and in the Hearts of Horror Lovers* (McFarland and Co., Publishers, Jefferson, NC, 1997)

Sutin, Lawrence, *Do What Thou Wilt: A Life of Aleister Crowley* (St. Martin's Griffin, 2002),

Svehla, Gary J. and Susan Svehla, (editors), *Midnight Marquee Actors Series: Bela Lugosi* and *Midnight Marquee*

Magazines

Mandell, Paul, "Edgar Ulmer and *The Black Cat*," *American Cinematographer* October 1984.

Roman, Robert C., "Boris Karloff," *Films in Review,* August/September 1964.

Rosar, William H., "Music for the Monsters," *The Quarterly Journal of the Library of Congress*, Fall 1983.

Weaver, Tom, "Shirley Ulmer," *Cult Movies*, #25.

"THE BLACK CAT" — A Universal Production PRINTED IN U S A

Lucifer Incarnate

Avenging Angel

David Manners and Jacqueline Wells, with the script for The Black Cat.

"Rapunzel, after a shopping spree at Frederick's of Hollywood." Lucille Lund as Karen

Harry Cording gave a barbaric quality to his portrayal of Thamal.

MANNERS and JACQUELINE WELLS in "THE BLACK CAT" — A UNIVERSAL PRODUCTION
PRINTED IN U. S. A.

David Manners as Peter Alison, and Jacqueline Wells as his bride, Joan - ill fated homeymooners.

"THE BLACK CAT" — A Universal Production PRINTED IN U.S.A.

"Every inch the gentleman" - *Jacqueline Wells' memory of Boris Karloff.*

"A delight, kind and considerate - *Jacqueline Wells' memory of Bela Lugosi.*

80

Karloff as Poelzig and Egon Brecher as his gnarled Majordomo. Brecher had been director of the Vienna Stadts Theater and a member of Eva Le Gallienne's Civic Repertory Company

The pivotal chess game.

"THE BLACK CAT" — A Universal Production   PRINTED IN U. S. A.

Lugosi as Werdegast, reflected in the table.

Karloff as Poelzig, and his reflection.

"THE BLACK CAT" — A Universal Production   PRINTED IN U. S. A.

The Rites of Lucifer - "Cum grano salis...!"

The red switch: "It has been a good game."

The winding stairs, to and from the Hellish cellar of Fort Mamaros

A very rare set shot, showing Fort Marmaros' Chart Room

The table where Werdegast selects the knife with which he skins Poelzig, revealing detail not glimpsed in the film itself.

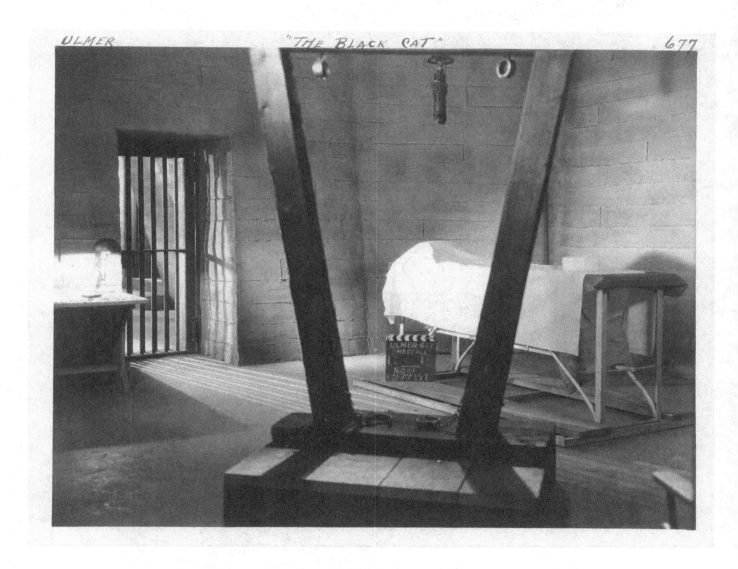

The rack where Werdegast will skin Poelzig alive, and the table where Werdegast will find the body of his murdered daughter Karen.

(All set stills courtesy of Ned Comstock, USC Performing Arts Library)

Lugosi and Henry Armetta.

Lugosi and Harry Cording.

90

David Manners and Jacqueline Wells.

"THE BLACK CAT" — A Universal Production   PRINTED IN U.S.A.

A trio of Universal Horror legends - David Manners, Boris Karloff and Bela Lugosi.

677-36

An unusual posed shot. As David Manners stands by, Lugosi dramatically grabs the desk statue of the naked woman that Karloff actually grasps as he watches the Alisons kiss. Meanwhile, note Karloff's sly smile, and the way he draws attention simply by the way he rests his left hand on the desk.

Comedy relief: Bela Lugosi, Boris Karloff, David Manners, Henry Armetta, and Albert Conti.

"THE BLACK CAT" — A Universal Production   PRINTED IN U S A.

Lugosi, Karloff, and Lucille Lund, as the corpse of Karen's mother.

Director Edgar G. Ulmer with Bela Lugosi, between scenes.

"The black cat is deathless...deathless as evil."

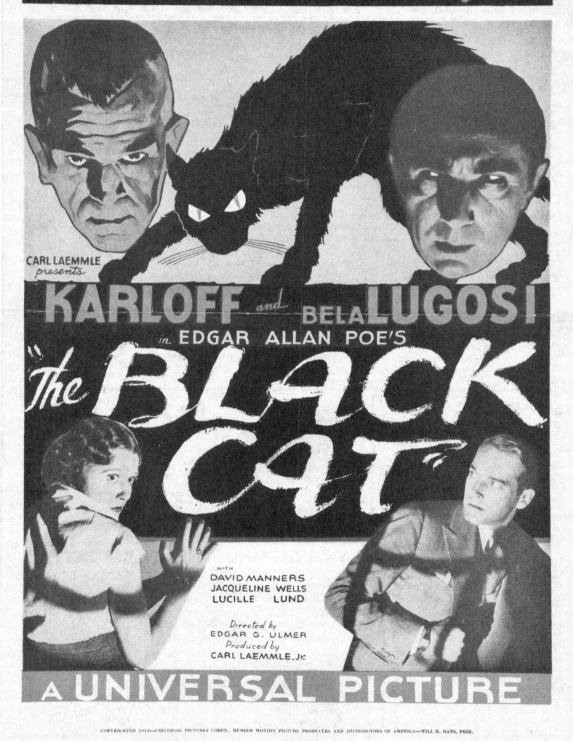

Pressbook Courtesy Ronald Borst/Hollywood Movie Poster

HERE IT IS!
THRILLER
OF THRILLERS
PRESENTING THREE
LADS WHO MADE GOOD!

KARLOFF

DAVID MANNERS

LUCILLE LUND

You have been hearing a lot about them. Now they are coming to your theatre—three little lads who made good.

"FRANKENSTEIN" Karloff known to showmen throughout the world as "Frankie."

"DRACULA" Lugosi, whom his exhibitor friends all call "Drac."

And the third lad, EDGAR ALLAN POE, whom everybody knows as "Eddie."

These three have made good in a tremonsterous way, and they are getting together for one picture to scare your patrons into fits of pleasure; to tickle them pink with goose pimples; to give them the most delightful jitters of their lives, and to make them love it !

If you are the showman we know you are, you are going to sell these cold-shiver boys the way you sold them before. There isn't a sissy in the trio. You won't want to soft-pedal on the thrills and chills and screams that they are ready to offer your folks. Don't play down the sensational angles — capitalize on them! Flash the town with sensational ballyhoo! Send your message searing through the city, cry to the skies that you have the biggest triple-barreled, non-stop, emotion-wrangler that ever stalked across a screen! Of course, if your people like romance, you can offer them romance. David Manners and Jacqueline Wells and Lucille Lund are all in the cast to give you the love angle, but first and foremost, put your faith and your hope and your bets on the big three in "The Black Cat" — KARLOFF, LUGOSI and POE! You can be sure that by not pussy-footing about them — you will fill to complete satisfaction, your house, your box-office, and the public's appetite for excitement. THE BLACK CAT is coming—sock it!

BELA LUGOSI

EDGAR ALLAN POE

JACQUELINE WELLS

ATMOSPHERIC SLIDE

Use the new effect slide, elaborate screen presentation on "The Black Cat." 3¼" x 4". For use with Brenograph F-7, positive alone will give excellent results, but with uncolored negative. colored, created especially for a made in two sizes 4" x 5" and standard equipment. The colored ater depth is obtained when used

PRICES:

4"x5"—Colored positive only	$2.00
—Set (positive and negative)	3.00
3¼"x4"—Colored positive only	1.50
Set (positive and negative)	2.25

Send remittance to avoid parcel post and C. O. D. charges.

Order direct from the NATIONAL STUDIOS, INC., 226 WEST 56th STREET, NEW YORK CITY, N. Y.

BLACK CAT TOYS FOR PRIZES!

Life-size fur cats with realistic black hair, as illustrated, are available for use as prizes or giveaways. Just the thing for a kiddies matinee, and adults would appreciate a gift like this too. Exhibit one in a showcase in your lobby under a green spot, and you will be sure to have plenty of people trying to win the contest for which it is an award. Price—$19.75 a dozen.

Order direct from the Capitol Novelty Company, 150 West 28th Street, New York City.

CAN YOU FIND "THE BLACK CAT?"

Use the above heading and plant the interesting puzzle illustrated on the right in your newspaper. Just tell the readers to black in all dotted sections and when they are all filled in, they will find "The Black Cat." A great feature for a children's page, or magazine section. Exploitation Service Mat BC No. 3 is available in 2 column size at your exchange.

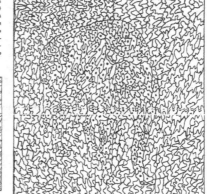

LOBBY— PERFECT OPPORTUNITY FOR SHOWMANSHIP! FLASH A SMASH FRONT!

GIANT BLACK CAT AND VIVID CUT-OUTS WILL STOP CROWDS!

Let passers-by know what you are showing. Build up a big front as illustrated—it need not be expensive. A giant compo board cat can be cut out as shown and placed over your entire box-office, reaching up to your overhead signs. Above entrance doors feature photos of Karloff and Lugosi with catch lines as shown. If possible, arrange for these heads to be situated in front of a shadow box, which will conceal pin point spot lights focused behind the eyes of the stars, give a weird effect.

For box-office, use heads of the minor players and also a placard reading as follows: "Beware of goose pimples, shivers, chills, scares—"BLACK CAT" will give you all of these, and if you can't take it, do not see this picture, but if you are a real thrill-lover, here is the sensation of a lifetime."

Take advantage of the poster cut-outs as illustrated and also the many fine accessories which are illustrated in other parts of this press book. Make your front a flash. You never had a finer chance than this for tremendous showmanship on a picture.

STUNTS WITH YOUR POSTER CUT-OUTS

There are several excellent opportunities to work with cut-outs on this picture inasmuch as the posters are filled with action, and the black cat is used as a predominating motif in the art work. The 3-sheet for example, can be silhouetted, the cat moved up two or three feet, its eyes cut out and a pin point spotlight focused on the figures below. The six-sheet can be handled in an equally effective way.

3-SHEET   6-SHEET CUT-OUT

COSTUMES FOR USHERS

The illustrations show a costume suitable for your ushers, doorman, or barker. Made of black sateen in small, medium and large sizes. Price, only $3.75 each.

Order direct from Valley Forge Flag Company, Spring City, Pa.

SHOWM

STARTLE THE TOWN WITH SNIPES

The series of three special teaser snipes reproduced above are 1/3 one sheet size, convenient for almost any open spot. This is a cracker-jack way to plaster the town in advance of the coming of your picture. "BLACK CAT" rates a big advance, and this is how to get it cheaply.

A few days ahead, get out these interest provoking snipes in your regular teasing campaign. Snipe empty walls, ash cans, regular locations, store windows, bulletin boards, in fact, every place possible. A really great way to sell the title, the stars, and the thrills. Snipes are available at your local Universal exchange. The size is 13x25 inches. Small imprint space is provided on the bottom of each. The price is low. Order in quantity.

ONLY 5c Each — 15c a Set

GIANT CAT BALLYHOO

For the costume illustrated below, use black cambric and have a local seamstress sew it up and your sign painter decorate it. Or perhaps a theatrical costumer can supply you with the outfit. It should be sufficiently large to accommodate two ballyhoo men, one for the front part of the cat, and one for the back.

In walking through the streets have these men cavort, leap and carry on in such a way as to attract extra attention. You can be certain of stopping crowds with this stunt. Have it out on the street a day or so in advance, and also through your entire showing.

carry on in such a way as to attract extra attention. You can be certain of stopping crowds with this stunt. Have it out on the street a day or so in advance, and also through your entire showing.

LUCK CHARMS

Tiny metal black cats, 3/4" size are available. These novelties can be strong and distributed with your house program or can be used for envelope stuffers, at your theatre. An inexpensive item with many uses. Price: $3.50 per M. Envelopes can be supplied with imprint for $1.50 a thousand additional. Order direct from the Universal uses Price: $3.50 per M. Envelopes can be supplied with imprint for $1.50 a thousand additional. Order direct from the Universal Toy and Novelty Company, 2329 Third Avenue, New York City.

CAPSULE GAG

Look up a local pharmaceutical jobber and have him supply you with several thousand small capsules. Imprint a display line for the BLACK CAT on a small piece of onion-skin paper and roll or fold this so it can be inserted into the capsule. Copy might be as follows:

"If you can't sleep nights, if your dreams are easily disturbed, if your nerves are bad, or your heart is weak, don't see the BLACK CAT, but if you enjoy a real thrill, by all means see the Karloff-Lugosi sensation at the Strand Theatre."

CAMPAIC

If you handled "DRACULA" or "FRANKENSTEIN," you know with power, sell it for what it is!

Use the frightened figure of a black cat with back upraised every bit of exploitation you do, sell Karloff, Lugosi and Poe tie-ups. Go after the big three.

1. KARLOFF—tie-up to his previous great screen triumph by his name. Use his face with its unusual make-up and sell the calling him "Frankenstein" Karloff everywhere, you mention fact that he is the greatest outstanding portrayer of uncanny screen characters since Lon Chaney. Mention his celebrated successes, "The Miracle Man," "THE MUMMY," "THE OLD DARK HOUSE," and "The Lost Patrol."

2. BELA LUGOSI—original creator of the role of "DRACULA" both on stage and screen. He is identified in the minds of millions of fans with these remarkable characterizations. Take advantage of the fact by billing him as "DRACULA" LUGOSI and use stills of him in awesome and eerie poses. Exploit his appearance for the first time with Karloff in the same picture, a tremendous exploitation angle.

SIDEWALK PROJECTOR

If you do not have in your equipment, a sidewalk projector, arrange to borrow one for your run of this picture. It will attract special attention to your showing.

Use a slide showing a prowling black cat with the shown. Rigged up under the marquee at night it will cause a crowd stopping mass on the sidewalk, or it can be used on your theatre wall or some adjacent building to good effect. Take advantage of this stunt for this picture. It's a natural.

TRAILER PRESENTATION

As a build-up for your trailer, or as a special announcement two weeks in advance, use the following presentation:

Extinguish all house lights except exit bulbs. Throw a slide of a giant black cat around the walls and on the curtain of your house, and simultaneously, through the amplifiers, sound terrific snarling, hissing, and cat calls. Use the following presentation:

Extinguish all house lights except exit bulbs. Throw a slide of a giant black cat around the walls and on the curtain of your house, and simultaneously, through the amplifiers, sound terrific snarling, hissing, and cat calls. This can be registered on a record cheaply for the purpose.

After about a half a minute, pick up a black cat on your stage with a green spot. This can be done by two men in a costume as described under the heading of "ballyhoo." Have this cat slink across the stage, raise its back, show its fangs, and then while the snarling is still going on, leap into the orchestra pit and vanish under the stage. You can follow this with your trailer or some other screen announcement, and create an impression that will have them talking for days.

SEND IN CAMPAIGNS

Please send me campaign details on this picture for reproduction in the Showmanship section of the Universal Weekly.

A. J. Sharick

DIRECTOR OF EXPLOITATION
Rockefeller Center, New York, N. Y.

WORD-COINING CONTEST

To describe a picture like the BLACK CAT, ordinary adjectives do not suffice. Explain that fact to the fans through your local newspaper and ask everyone to submit coined words that will succeed in selling the fascination, thrill, chill, entertainment and other features of this remarkable Edgar Allan Poe thriller. Such words for example as TREMONSTEROUS will do the trick. Ask for other suggestions. Offer passes as prizes for the best words submitted.

SCREAMS MAKE TALK

It will be a good idea, at least for the first few showings of BLACK CAT to plant a few women in the audience with instructions to scream at certain highspots of the picture. Screams put the audience into the right mood for enjoyment of the picture and also serve to start word-of-mouth advertising, which spreads like wild fire and reacts to the benefit of the box-office.

NOVELTY CARDS

Tie up with your local drug store for a sufficient supply of court plaster to be attached to several thousand cards to read: Here Is Your Court Plaster. Use It On Your Lips To Keep From Screaming When You See "BLACK CAT." This succeeds in selling the thriller from a humorous angle and should be used in addition to other exploitation that stresses the thrills.

Here is your **COURT PLASTER**
(COMPLIMENTS OF MAIN ST. DRUG STORE)

KARLOFF in Edgar Allan Poe's **BLACK "CAT"** with BELA DRACULA LUGOSI

AD GAG

Tie-up with your local classified advertising editor, who is always on the lookout for stunts that will call attention to his section. Have him put an ad under the heading of "Lost and Found," reading as follows:

LOST

In the columns of the classified ads today, the BLACK CAT is lost! That is, the letters in "BLACK CAT" appear scattered through several of the other ads. If you can locate the BLACK CAT by finding the ads, which contain all the letters, submit them to the classified ad editor. For the first ten received, free passes will be given to see the new Karloff-Lugosi sensation, "BLACK CAT," now at the Strand Theatre.

ILLUMINA

CAT'S PAW STENCIL

Stenciling the streets is advisable to announce this picture, and you can get a wax stencil made up at little cost. To vary the stunt a trifle, spot Karloff and "BLACK CAT" at intervals as shown. Use water colors for the purpose and you will avoid trouble with the authorities. Red and black are the best colors for this stunt.

KARLOFF BLACK CA

...ANSHIP!

...N PLAN

know what to do with the "BLACK CAT." Sell it with punch,

and hair-standing-on-end as atmosphere in all advertising, so that they deserve to be sold on the basis of tremendous reputa...

1. EDGAR ALLAN POE—immortal author of the weirdest, most fantastic tales that ever came from the mind of man. His reputation is world-wide. His stories are classics, used in every language. This picture is based on one of his most unusual yarns and you should use his name for everything it is worth.

The balance of the cast includes many players with considerable followings. David Manners, handsome young leading man; Jacquline Wells, pretty and popular player; Andy Devine, a natural comedian; Herman Bing, buffoon, who will become a big word for comedy; Lucille Lund, All American girl, and Wampas baby star.

EDGAR ULMER, director of "BLACK CAT," will establish himself as an unusual genius with his innovations and masterful touches, which help make this picture an entertainment sensation. Use his name and build a box-office asset.

SNAPSHOT CONTEST

Cooperate with your local developing-printing shops, or camera accessory shops, for a snapshot contest open to everyone in town. The only requirement is that the snapshot shall register a person expressing the jitters. This can be either comedy stuff, which will show someone with hair on end, or serious facial expressions, but in all events must indicate that the subject has been tremendously startled. Call the contest a "BLACK CAT" Camera Test.

To the best photograph of this type, award a camera or similar prize...

LOBBY EXHIBIT

Most people are superstitious and that is what will make a display of this type outstandingly unusual to hold your interest.

In a corner of your lobby, or within the house, properly spotlighted, fix up the following artifacts: A short ladder, leaning against the wall; a large calendar date, Friday, 13th, tacked on to it; an open umbrella from one of the runes, and underneath the ladder, a fierce-looking toy black cat and a hair-sized mirror smashed to bits; a sign with rope, as shown, completes the display.

Superstitious?
KARLOFF in "BLACK CAT" is COMING!
FRI. 13
GOOD LUCK for ALL...LOVERS!

POE SCHOOL TIE-UP

Because of the tremendous reputation which Edgar Allan Poe enjoys, his works are used in many literature classes throughout American schools. Under the circumstances, tie-ups with the showing of your picture should be easily arranged.

Contact principals or teachers in your locality and arrange for visits of pupils to see the picture in groups, or to stimulate extra interest, sponsor an essay contest on the subject of Edgar Allan Poe's life or why "BLACK CAT" can be considered one of his most outstanding masterpieces. Be sure that bulletins or cards announcing your showing appear in every school and at spots patronized by school children.

...TED CAT'S HEAD

Have your sign painter create the most ferocious looking head of a black cat possible, copying as much as possible the style of the one reproduced here. The eyes should be cut out and red rims painted around. In place of the eyes themselves, photos of Karloff and Lugosi mounted on transparencies. Behind these transparencies, dimmer bulbs or flashes can make the cat open or close its eyes or blink rapidly, creating a line effect that will stop every passer-by. This is a great stunt for over or under the marquee, or your lobby. It will also make an excellent shadow-box.

T...STRAND

PROMOTE LOCAL BLACK CAT SHOW

"BLACK CAT" PRIZE SHOW
ENTRIES
AWARDS
Most Beautiful "Black Cat"
Weirdest "Black Cat"
Biggest "Black Cat"
STRAND THEATRE

FRANKENSTEIN KARLOFF and "DRACULA" LUGOSI in Edgar Allan Poe's BLACK CAT

The first black cat show on record was held in Universal City for the purpose of selecting a cat to appear in the picture and the stunt was a tremendous success.

This gives you a cue for a great stunt that should arouse local interest and get plenty of space in the columns of your papers. Announce a black cat show to be staged in your theatre with prizes going to the biggest, most beautiful, and weirdest-looking specimens. Winners can be given prize ribbons and by co-operating with a pet shop, it will be possible to get merchandise or other awards for the contestants. In every case, the cat can be treated to a big bowl of milk, and the young-ster who brings him or her given a pass to see the show. Be sure to notify newspapers of this event, and have reporters and photographers present. You might also get the local branch of the S. P. C. A. interested and use names of cat fanciers in town as sponsors. This can be a really big and unusual stunt if properly promoted. Should it be impractical in your town for any reason, you can at least sponsor a black cat snapshot contest asking people in town to submit photos of their cats of that color, and put them on view in your lobby with prizes for various specimens as described above. By all means do something along this line and cash in on an unusual angle.

TWO NEWSPAPER ART CONTESTS

Art contests always receive a fine response and for that reason, two of them are offered here, both single enough so that anyone can participate whether or not possessing drawing ability.

BLACK CAT TITLE CONTEST

The sketch illustrated at the upper left is available in mat form (Exploitation Service Mat No. BC—1) and should be planted in your local paper. It shows, as you see, a black cat entirely constructed from the letters in the title. Ask contestants to submit their pictures of the black cat drawn in the same way, but in different positions. For the best creation of this type award some suitable prize.

MONSTER CUT-OUT CONTEST

The second contest consists of three heads, Karloff, Lugosi, and the "Black Cat," and from this a monster must be constructed who is more terribly and forbidding than any of the individual pictures. The silhouette shown at the right is but example of one such creation. There are numerous others possible by cutting the heads in various ways to secure the proper effect. A mat is available of the three heads mentioned and also the other reproduction. Ask at your exchange for Exploitation Service Mat BC-2.

EXP. SERV. MAT BC No. 1

EXPLOITATION SERVICE MAT BC No. 2

ATMOSPHERIC CAT NOVELTIES!

A number of lobby and marquee hangers are available to create atmosphere in your lobby for the showing of "BLACK CAT." These are not imprinted, but can be hung around your marquee boxoffice and theatre walls. Have the eyes cut out and suspend pieces for extra effects. Please note that this material is merely for special atmosphere and cannot be considered as taking the place of the regular line of exploitation accessories which are reproduced on other pages of this press book. Order any of the following, by number direct from the distributor.

No. 1—JOINTED CAT

Die-cut of heavy cardboard, with red mouth and green eyes. The tail and four legs are eyeletted to the body and are movable. String with cord for easy hanging. Size is 16x24 inches. $.12 each.

No. 2—CAT STREAMER

Die-cut streamer made of heavy cardboard, 6 cats to each streamer, of six feet (each cat being one foot). The tails are eyeletted to the bodies and can be moved into various positions. String with cord for easy hanging. Price per streamer $.12 each.

No. 3—EMBOSSED CAT HEAD

Cat head size 12x12 inches, made of heavy cardboard. Embossed and die-cut with string at top. The eyes and mouth can be cut out at your theatre, and covered with red or green tissue paper or cellophane; and hang before a bright light for spooky effect. Price $.10 each.

No. 4—EMBOSSED CAT FIGURE

Large figure of a cat size 12x18 inches, die-cut and embossed, with string at top for hanging. Eyes and mouth can be cut out and covered with red or green tissue paper or cellophane for spooky effect. Price $.08 each.

An assortment of the above may be ordered at $2.50, $5.00 or $10.00.

Order direct from
ECONOMY NOVELTY & PRINTING COMPANY
239 West 39th Street, New York City

STYLE No. 4

STYLE No. 3

STYLE No. 1

ACCESSORIES

EVERY ITEM IS A SENSATIONAL SALES-AID! USE THEM!

OO-OO-OO-OO!

DOES THAT HERALD SELL?

SIZE 8" x 9½"
(FLAT)

RED and GREEN COVER
PURPLE INSIDE!

PRICE

$3.00 per M

ORDER DIRECT FROM YOUR LOCAL UNIVERSAL EXCHANGE

A STRIKING 2 COLOR — 15 FOOT FLASH!

DIE-CUT AND STRUNG $2.50 EACH AT UNIVERSAL EXCHANGE

TWO — 22 x 28s

14 x 36 INSERT

EIGHT — 11 x 14s

SLIDE

SELL IT

THE WAY IT SHOULD BE SOLD – – USE EXTRA QUANTITIES – ORDER EARLY!

ABOVE—ONE SHEET "B"
CENTER—THREE SHEET "C"
RIGHT—ONE SHEET "D"

NOTE – Colors on 24 - Sheet are as follows: background, green - heads, purple and blues - cat, black - cat's eyes, yellow - title, white.

IMPRINT SPACE

USE TWO
OF THESE
WINDOW CARDS
IN EVERY LOCATION
– GET THEM COMING AND GOING!

FLASH HANGER EVERYWHERE

2 COLORS
DIE-CUT
AND
STRUNG

PRICE
15c
EACH

GET YOUR TRAILER EARLY!

It's unusual! Full of thrills to make them gasp and wonder and want to see more!

Order Direct From

NATIONAL SCREEN SERVICE

630 Ninth Ave., New York; 810 So. Wabash Ave., Chicago, Ill.; 300½ So. Harwood St., Dallas, Texas; 1922 So. Vermont Ave., Los Angeles, Calif., 2418 Second Ave., Seattle, Wash.

THIS STILL
IS IN YOUR EXCHANGE SET. USE IT FOR CHESS TIE-UPS—A PASTIME MORE POPULAR NOW THAN EVER—PLANT IT ON COUNTERS AND IN WINDOWS!

ORDER DIRECT FROM YOUR UNIVERSAL EXCHANGE

EGON BRECHER and JACQUELINE WELLS in "THE BLACK CAT" UNIVERSAL PRODUCTION

Cut "E"

Scene from "THE BLACK CAT" UNIVERSAL PRODUCTION

Cut "D"

BELA LUGOSI and JACQUELINE WELLS in "THE BLACK CAT" UNIVERSAL PRODUCTION

Cut "F"

KARLOFF in "The BLACK CAT" UNIVERSAL PRODUCTION

Cut "A"

For the Program

YOU all remember "Franken-stein!"
And can you forget "Dracula?" Now, they clash together, with a horrifying impact in Universal's master-thriller, "The Black Cat," with Karloff ("Frankenstein") and Bela Lugosi ("Dracula"), starting on ———— at this theatre.

Karloff sent the chills up your spine in Frankenstein and Lugosi chased them down again in "Dracula," now the two together will amaze and mystify you.

Two dead souls come to life after a lapse of many years, with a lustful desire to wreck vengeance upon each other. An innocent young couple, just married, and on their honeymoon, become involved in their sinister machinations.

It packs a terrific wallop and is crammed full of fantastic situations.

Karloff and Lugosi are unforgettable in this picture, while David Manners and Jacqueline Wells supply an unusual romantic team, who will make you laugh and cry with them.

Stay away from all black cats until you see Karloff and Lugosi in "The Black Cat."

Remember the day is ————
And the place is ————
Be prepared for the thrill of your lives!

At A Glance

Title ———— "THE BLACK CAT"
Brand ———— Universal Production
Stars ———— Karloff and Bela Lugosi
Screenplay by ———— Peter Ruric
Based on the Story by ———— Edgar Allan Poe
Directed by ———— Edgar Ulmer
Photographed by ———— John Mescal
Time ———— The Present
Place ———— Central Europe

The Cast

Poelzig	KARLOFF
Dr. Verdegast	BELA LUGOSI
Peter	David Manners
Joan	Jacqueline Wells
Karen	Lucille Lund
Majordomo	Egon Brecher
Maid	Anna Duncan
Car Steward	Herman Bing
Train Conductor	Andre Cheron
Train Steward	Luis Alberni
Thamal	Harry Cording
Bus Driver	George Davis
Porter	Alphonse Martell
Border Patrolman	Tony Marlow
Station Master	Paul Weigel
Waiter	Albert Polet
Brakeman	Rodney Hildebrand

JACQUELINE WELLS in "The BLACK CAT" UNIVERSAL PRODUCTION

Cut "B"

Two Fiends Clash in Death Struggle

While Black Cat Creeps

(Advance Story)

COULD "Frankenstein" have defeated "Dracula" in mortal combat? The issue has finally been put to a test by Universal Pictures, which brought together for the first time on the screen, those two terror inspiring "monsters," Karloff and Lugosi, in a horror picture that promises to end all horror pictures, "The Black Cat," starting on ———— at this theatre.

A gripping story, full of unusual and unexpected thrills and chills, in "The Black Cat," coming to the ———— Theatre, on ————

Karloff, the creator of "Franken-stein" and "Dracula," it is said, promises to outdo both "Franken-stein" and "Dracula," it is said. Karloff, the creator of "Franken-stein" takes on a new guise of hor-rible and terrorizing proportions, while Lugosi, the originator of "Dracula" braves the laws of life and death when he clashes with his sinister adversary.

No picture in recent times has evoked so much interest among the theatre going public, who are al-ways seeking something new and daringly different in screen enter-tainment. That picture is more than that; it is truly an epic of fantastic horror and terror.

A splendid cast has been as-sembled for this production, in-cluding David Manners and Jac-queline Wells, who supply the ro-mantic interest; Egon Brecher, Lucille Lund, Henry Armetta, Anna Duncan, Harry Cording and many others.

Poelzig and Dr. Verdegast, por-trayed by Karloff and Lugosi re-spectively, are old-world characters of sinister, mysterious bearing, yet carrying on their deadly machina-tions in this present day among very modern young people. They seem like reincarnated throw-backs of another age, and their deviltries make "Frankenstein" and "Drac-ula" appear like mere practical jokers.

BELA LUGOSI in "The BLACK CAT" UNIVERSAL PRODUCTION

Cut "C"

"The Black Cat" Outthrills "Frankenstein" and "Dracula" Together

When Monsters Meet

(Advance Story)

ALTHOUGH they have both been in Hollywood for many years and have portrayed similar types of roles on the screen many times, neither Karloff nor Bela Lugosi, those two "terror" stars, had ever met before they were in-troduced on the set of "The Black Cat" at Universal studio.

It was just one of those strange coincidences Hollywood is noted for and both men had a hearty chuckle over it when they shook hands for the first time, each with an interesting past, expecting to see them glare at each other, con-sidering that Karloff was the or-iginal creator of "Frankenstein" and Lugosi the lurid "vampire" of "Dracula."

What actually happened was that both men bowed courteously and smiled broadly over a warm hand-clasp.

It is of course the first time these two screen demons have ever ap-peared together in the same pic-ture, which is said to be remark-ably unique and even more thrilling than either "Frankenstein" or "Dracula."

Returns to Life
After Twenty Years
in A Prison Camp

(Advance Story)

FOLLOWING the last great war, countless thousands of men, taken prisoners on the outskirts of civilization, and whose coun-tries' governments were obliter-ated, were never released until many years later. Among these as ill-fated and twenty years elapsed before these unfortunates regained their freedom.

It is easy to understand what suffering and torture these men must have gone through. Their very souls were killed, their bodies seared and mutilated, until death impungled over life. Very few ever returned alive from this "Death Hell," but those who did were nev-ver the same again. They were as a Living death from the dead Life no longer interested and contempt for their fellow men and passion seemed them and an evil passion seemed to possess them.

Such a human creature is vividly described in "The Black Cat," a vital's epic of the "Theatre." These two outstanding "horror" stars Karloff, the monster of "Franken-stein" and Bela Lugosi, the vam-pire of "Dracula," combine that terrific talents to make this one a the weirdest films ever made. Edgar Ulmer directed.

"The Black Cat" Set in Central Europe

(Advance Feature)

A vivid pictorial description of some of the most picturesque and out of the way spots in Central Europe, where many legends of mystery have sprung up, is given in Universal's thriller, "The Black Cat," coming to the ———— Theatre on ————

The same locale from which the sinister "vampire" of "Dracula" was alleged to have come, on the out-skirts of Hungary, is painted with glowing pictures in this film, which is based on a tale of the same name by Edgar Allan Poe.

Some of the unusual scenic photography includes that of the famous Fort Marmaros, which was completely ruined during the World War, then rehabilitated. It was on this spot where ten thou-sand men died in one day in one of the most gruesome battles of the war.

The fort still stands today, with much of its original features still alive. An iron fortified artillery room, a steel girded atelier and a dungeon, once famous for its tor-turous atmosphere is still preserved and faithfully depicted in the picture.

A terrific rainstorm, with start-ling effects, provides one of the thrilling moments in the story which climaxes with a sound-shattering explosion, laying barren a whole countryside.

Karloff and Lugosi, those thrill-ing portrayers of "Frankenstein" and "Dracula," are brought to ————

Bela Lugosi Once
Played Romeo!

(Advance Story)

A New Creature Joins The Karloff Parade
of Monsters in "The Black Cat"

(Advance Story)

THE art of make-up is one of the greatest creations of the screen. Proper or improper make-up often "makes" or "breaks" an actor's performance. One of Hollywood's greatest authorities on make-up is Jack Pierce, Universal studio's head of that department. In the fifteen or more years he has been with the company Pierce has "made-up" literally countless hundreds of actors and actresses. It was Pierce who first devised and created the hor-rible plastique make-up Lon Chaney used to wear in his weird roles.

His creation of the mask-like bulging face of the horrible Quasi-modo in "The Hunchback of Notre Dame," together with Chaney's

"Jiggs" Wins Prize
at Black Cat Show

(Advance Story)

ONE of the oddest contests e

The Magnetism of Hollywood Drew

The Story of "The Black Cat"

PETER and Joan Alison, newlyweds, are travelling by train on their honeymoon to a European resort. A sombre and sinister looking stranger boards the train. It seems that a mistake has been made. This man has purchased space in their compartment. Peter is polite and invites the stranger to share their room.

The stranger introduces himself as Dr. Verdegast, whose past seems to be shrouded in mystery, now on his way to visit an old friend, Hjalmar Poelzig.

As they are all going near the same destination they get off at the next station and engage a bus to transport them the rest of the way. It is a miserable, stormy, night. On the way the bus crashes and turns over. The driver is killed and Joan is hurt and unconscious. Peter and Verdegast, aided by Thamal, the latter's servant and bodyguard, carry Joan to Poelzig's house which is nearby.

Verdegast sends for Poelzig and proceeds to attend to Joan's injuries, finally inducing her to sleep. Poelzig comes in, looking strange and morbid. When he greets Verdegast it is evident a feeling of strong animosity exists between the two men.

Verdegast tells Poelzig he has returned for Karen, his wife, from whom fate had separated him all these years. Poelzig attempts to evade the subject and Verdegast becomes hostile, when Peter enters the room and interrupts them.

The three men drink some wine, when Verdegast suddenly pales, his glass falling to the floor. Directly ahead of him stands a big black cat. He hurls a knife at it. At that moment Joan comes out of her bedroom as though in a trance. A sudden change has come over her. She is curiously bold and alive. Peter persuades her to go back to her room and is worried. Verdegast admits his phobia for black cats and tells Peter of the ancient superstition which claims the black cat is the living embodiment of evil and at death that evil enters into the nearest living being. Poelzig with an immobile expression, says the black cat does not die.

They all retire for the night and Peter is disturbed by the strange atmosphere of the house and at the actions of Verdegast and Poelzig. The latter two resume their discussion about Verdegast's wife. Poelzig takes him to a curious chamber where he tells him that his wife died many years ago and her child—a girl—is also dead. Verdegast becomes menacing but is stopped by the snarl of another cat.

The next morning Joan is seemingly recovered from her ill effects of the accident. Two gendarmes arrive to obtain an account of the accident and enliven the atmosphere a bit with their humorous dialogue.

Peter and Joan decide to depart but discover they cannot get out of the house. In a struggle Peter is knocked out and Joan taken back to her room at Poelzig's orders.

Joan tries to escape and stumbles into another room where she discovers a beautiful girl, Karen, the daughter of Verdegast, and now the wife of Poelzig. She warns Joan to get out of the house before it is too late.

Verdegast, told by Joan of his daughter's presence, is enraged at this news and vows vengeance on Poelzig. The two men meet and there is a desperate struggle. Joan and Peter manage to get out of the ill-fated house, leaving Poelzig and Verdegast in mortal combat.

(Advance Story)

THE grim starkness of "Frankenstein" and the cold chills of "Dracula" were but delightful pranks, compared to the weird and uncanny theme of "The Black Cat," Universal's master horror picture opening at the ________ Theatre on ________

Imagine if you can, the first time on the screen together, Karloff, the monster of "Frankenstein" and Bela Lugosi, the vampire of "Dracula."

Together they will make you tremble and shiver.

Two demons in human guise meet on the ground of ten thousand dead souls. Grim hatred and bitter revenge flame their hearts as they clash in what seems immortal combat.

Two innocent young lovers, blissfully unaware of their danger, are caught in the satanic toils of these two blood frozen creatures and made the unwilling victims of dread and fear.

Never before has such rank terror and fright been presented on the screen. Replete with thrills and fraught with chills "The Black Cat" will astound you with its daring.

Based on that famed tale of Edgar Allan Poe, America's greatest mystery writer, this picture is said to be the last word in melodramatic thrills. It abounds with intense suspense, intrigue and super-dramatic highlights.

A great supporting cast has been assembled to make this one of the outstanding pictures of the year and includes Jacqueline Wells, David Manners, Egon Brecher, Herman Bing and Lucille Lund.

Dame," together with Chaney's sympathetic portrayal of this pitiable gnomelike creature, will remain one of the classic contributions to screen history. Chaney's "Phantom of the Opera" make-up, hat of the mad musician, Eric, who haunted the subterranean recesses of the Paris Opera House, was another of Pierce's memorable jobs.

Pierce was also on hand to help Conrad Veidt along the path of cinema horror with his hideous leering grin of Gwymplaine in "The Man Who Laughs" when Universal produced this Victor Hugo classic.

But of all the screen actors he has molded and reshaped, Pierce believes the most unusual and readily adaptable of them all is Karloff, whom he designates the "master of make-up." Karloff, he says, has the most unique physiognomy of any actor either on stage or screen. His features are so pliably shaped it can be changed and altered at a moment's notice with a few dabs of grease and paint.

Pierce considers his greatest accomplishment the make-up he originated and created for Karloff in "Frankenstein." It was entirely his own conception of what the "monster" looked like.

Karloff's most recent gargoylish adventure into the realms of horror and mystery takes place in "The Black Cat," a daringly different and distinctly thrilling picture, suggested by Edgar Allan Poe's noted tale. With Karloff is Bela Lugosi, the creator of the "vampire" in "Dracula." This will be the first time the two are together on the screen.

O[illegible] staged in Hollywood was Universal studio's Black Cat sh[illegible] [illegible] at the studio during the making of "The Black Cat," the horror thriller with Karloff and Lugosi coming to the ________ Theatre next ________

More than five hundred cats, ranging from the common, every-day variety alley cat to prize Angoras and Persians flocked to the studio from all parts of the city to participate in the big event.

After a hard fought competitive battle, in which a number of casualties, such as a few scratched eyes, took place, the first prize went to a fierce looking Persian puss who answered to the name of "Jiggs." A contract to appear in the picture went with the award and "Jiggs" is now the most famous black cat in the country.

If you've often wondered where the expression "Catty" came from you should have been at the Black Cat party and watched those felines vie with each for attention. "Jiggs" later claimed he only won by a "cat's whisker," so there you are.

Karloff and Lugosi acted as the judges of the contest and had a pretty difficult time of it before they picked the winner. Everyone was satisfied when it was all over. The cats had enough cream and their children owners were supplied with all the ice cream they could guzzle without making themselves ill.

"The Black Cat" will be seen at the ________ Theatre starting ________ The cast supporting Karloff and Lugosi includes David Manners, Lucille Lund, Egon Brecher, Anna Duncan, Harry Cording, Luis Alberni, and Henry Armetta. Edgar Ulmer directed.

([illegible])

HOLLYWOOD is the land of "types." A screen actor becomes identified with the characterization of a certain role and thereafter must abide by his type.

Perhaps one of the greatest examples of this theory can be found in Bela Lugosi, who as Count Dracula in the unforgettable stage and screen versions of "Dracula," definitely typed himself as a weird, fantastic character. In "The Black Cat" he carries on the tradition.

But Lugosi was not always the dark and sinister "heavy." At the age of twenty he made his stage debut as "Romeo" in a Hungarian production of "Romeo and Juliet" and followed it with three years of Shakespearean repertoire, Ibsen and other classics.

When he came to America his first English speaking role was in "The Red Poppy," where he played a Spanish Apache. Alan Dale, the late dean of New York critics, later said of him: "He's the greatest actor ever to come to America."

After years of straight and romantic leads Lugosi found himself playing the unearthy character of the vampire in "Dracula." His performance over two years in New York and six months on the road, was so realistic, so forceful, he has remained "Dracula" to this day. It was this characterization that proved the sesame to his screen career.

Lugosi comes to the ________ Theatre next ________ with Karloff in Universal's "The Black Cat," with David Manners, Jacqueline Wells, Lucille Lund and other players.

Karloff and Lugosi from Foreign Lands

(Advance Feature)

THE screen is perhaps the greatest medium of expression known It is also the giant magnete that attracts every type of people, from all walks of life and from all ends of the world. Men and women, whose ordinary, natural course in life would probably never cross, are brought together in Hollywood under the glaring eye of the camera.

Consider the strange coincidence that served to bring together those two noted character exhibitionists of the screen—Karloff, that great master of make-up and creator of that horrible "monster," "Frankenstein," and Bela Lugosi, whose unforgetaable "Dracula," will go down in the archives of motion picture history.

Karloff, a quiet and reserved Englishman, started out in life as a studious, academic person, whose father wanted him to prepare for the British Consular service. Lugosi, on the other hand, was always a firebrand, engaged in political activity in his native Hungary until he was forced to flee to America for safety. Since then, he has lived only by and for his profession.

Following entirely different paths, yet these two men eventually arrival at the same place. And finally they are to appear in the same picture together.

"The Black Cat," Universal's super-thriller, with both Karloff and Lugosi, comes to the ________ Theatre on ________, with a splendid cast that includes David Manners, Jacqueline Wells, Lucille Lund, Egon Brecher, Harry Cording, Henry Armetta, Albert Conti and others. Edgar Ulmer, a protege of Max Rheinhardt, directed.

Advance Notes

Some of the most exciting scenes in "The Black Cat," coming to the ________ Theatre next ________ was taken in a blinding rainstorm. Rain is not a "usual" phenomenon in California, but this particular night it was raining "cats and dogs" well, anyway, "cats." No less than a half dozen black cats were used in this production, which brings together Karloff and Lugosi for the first time on the screen, or as they are known to millions of fans, "Frankenstein" and "Dracula." Edgar Ulmer directed.

* * *

The greatest master of make-up since the immortal Lon Chaney, yet Karloff, who comes to the ________ Theatre in "The Black Cat," Universal's super-thriller, would prefer playing straight leading roles if his fans would let him.

It wasn't until he created the "monster" in "Frankenstein" that Karloff became identified with horror characterizations, which made it imperative for him to don hideous make-up. In "The Black Cat," it is not so much his make-up as his startling interpretation that inspires fear and terror.

* * *

It was almost a herculean feat for Harry Cording, who plays the massive servant in "The Black Cat," Universal's super thriller, to lift David Manners in his arms almost as if he were a child. The stunt was even more remarkable considering that Manners is over six feet tall and weighs nearly 200 pounds. "The Black Cat," starring Karloff of "Frankenstein" fame, and Bela Lugosi ("Dracula") comes to the ________ Theatre next ________, with Jacqueline Wells, Lucille Lund, Egon Brecher, Henry Armetta and Albert Conti.

* * *

A courageous young lady is Jacqueline Wells, feminine lead in "The Black Cat," the Universal thriller coming to the ________ Theatre next ________ In one of the difficult scenes of the picture Miss Wells was required to go wading through a sea of mud. It was an expert bit of realism and one in which a "double" could not be used. Miss Wells went through the ordeal without flinching, but remained in her bath tub for two days thereafter.

* * *

Ever since he has been a motion picture actor, Bela Lugosi, who made himself famous as "Dracula," has had his own chair on every set he has worked. The chair is now over five years old and still in good condition.

Lugosi is featured in Universal's master thriller, "The Black Cat," starring Karloff ("Frankenstein") which comes to the ________ Theatre on ________ with Jacqueline Wells, David Manners, Lucille Lund and others in the cast.

* * *

Lucille Lund, "The All American Girl," won that title in a contest staged by Universal Pictures and College Humor Magazine. She was also awarded a contract by the studio.

Miss Lund comes to the ________ Theatre next ________ in Universal's thriller, "The Black Cat," with Karloff and Lugosi of "Frankenstein" and "Dracula' 'fame.

* * *

What would happen if "Frankenstein" and "Dracula" met?

Well, they did, and shook hands! Karloff, the star of "Frankenstein" and Bela Lugosi the creator of "Dracula," met for the first time, actually, on the set of "The Black Cat" at Universal City. They smiled at each other, bowed and shook hands. "The Black Cat," bringing together Karloff and Lugosi for the first time on the screen, comes to the ________ Theatre next ________

* * *

Harry Cording, who plays the part of Thamal, the sinister giant in "The Black Cat," Universal's thriller, coming to the ________ Theatre on ________, was once a noted football player at Rugby College, where he was educated. He is best remembered for his work with Emil Jannings in "The Patriot." Although a New York City native, Cording has played almost every type of role in as many nationalities.

Beware! "The Black Cat" Is Coming Soon

(Story on Booking)

ONE of the most unusual pictures of the season, bringing with it all the uncanny mystery and horror of "Frankenstein" and "Dracula," plus the added thrills supplied by those two creators of eerie roles—Karloff and Bela Lugosi, has been announced for an early showing at the ________ Theatre, according to Manager ________

It's Universal's master thriller, "The Black Cat," suggested from a story by Edgar Allan Poe, one of America's immortal mystery writers.

If you can imagine the monster of "Frankenstein" and the vampire of "Dracula" together on the screen for the first time, it will give you an idea what thrills and chills are in store for you.

Never before has such a daring photoplay been attempted, bringing together the screen's two greatest portrayers of horror roles, Karloff and Lugosi.

An expectancy of something new—different—long desired by film patrons, is justly promised by Universal for "The Black Cat." David Manners and Jacqueline Wells head the romantic leads, with Egon Brecher and Lucille Lund comprising but part of a great supporting cast.

Brief Biographies of the Principal Players in "The Black Cat"

KARLOFF

KARLOFF, the greatest portrayer of weird and uncanny screen characters since Lon Chaney, comes ________ to the ________ Theatre in "The Black Cat," the weird thriller based on the Edgar Allan Poe story. Despite his Russian sounding name he is a pronounced Britisher and was born in Dulwich, suburb of London, England. As "Frankenstein," he was immortalized on the screen. Since then he has appeared in "The Miracle Man," "The Mummy," "The Old Dark House," and "The Lost Patrol." Karloff is happily married to a non-professional and in real life is the direct opposite of his screen characterizations.

Cut "G"

BELA LUGOSI

BELA LUGOSI, the creator of Count Dracula in both the stage and screen versions of "Dracula," is is ideally mated with Karloff in "The Black Cat," coming on ________ to the ________ Theatre. It is based on the weird tale by Edgar Allan Poe. Lugosi is a native Hungarian, having been born in Lugos, Hungary, Oct. 20, 1884, the son of Baron Lugosi, banker. He came to America in 1921. Lugosi has appeared on the stage of two continents, being acclaimed as one of the greatest character delineators of this generation. His recent pictures include "Murders of the Rue Morgue," "A Kiss Before the Mirror." More recently he was featured in Earl Carroll's New York production, "Murder at the Vanities."

Cut "H"

JACQUELINE WELLS

JACQUELINE WELLS, a Wampas Baby Star of 1934, started in pictures as a serial queen only a year and a half ago and has made such rapid strides since that Universal rewarded her with the feminine lead in "The Black Cat," with Karloff and Bela Lugosi starred, which is coming ________ to the ________ Theatre. Her recent screen roles include the ingenue lead in "Tillie and Gus," "Alice's sister in "Alice in Wonderland" and "Tarzan the Fearless." She was born in Denver, Colo., August 30th, but was raised in Dallas, Tex., and Los Angeles, where she was educated at Kenwood Hall and studied dancing with Theodore Karloff and singing with Virginia Flohri. She can speak French and Spanish fluently. Miss Wells has brown hair and eyes.

Cut "I"

DAVID MANNERS

DAVID MANNERS, long considered one of the best of the younger screen leading men, has had a successful career on the stage and in films. His home town is Halifax, Canada. He moved to New York as a child with his parents and was educated at Trinity High School. He graduated from the University of Toronto. His first stage work was in "Dancing Mothers." Later he appeared with the Theatre Guild. His screen career started with "Journey's End." Manners married to Suzanne Bushnell, an Arizona girl. Among his recent pictures are "Roman Scandals," "Torch Singer," "The Devil's Love,, and "Dead on Arrival."

Cut "J"

LUCILLE LUND

LUCILLE LUND, coming to the ________ Theatre in support of Karloff and Lugosi in Universal's "The Black Cat," is a Wampas Baby Star of 1934, as is Jacqueline Wells, also in "The Black Cat." Miss Lund, "The All American Girl," entered pictures as the winner of the Universal-College Humor Magazine contest, after being acclaimed the most beautiful and talented of 1200 co-eds competing in the contest. Her first picture was "Saturday's Millions," followed by "Pirate Treasure." She is 5 ft. 4½ inches tall, weighs 114 pounds, has blonde hair and blue eyes.

Cut "K"

Boy! You Have Plenty To Sell In This Mystery —

IT'S TREMONSTROUS!

Because the monster of "Frankenstein" is in it! Because the monster of "Dracula" is in it! Because the eerie imagination of EDGAR ALLAN POE is in it!

THE BLACK CAT

KARLOFF and BELA LUGOSI

in the most thrilling story of unheard-of wickedness the screen has ever known! . . . A girl in the clutches of a monster who would preserve her beauty forever! Her lover battling he knew not what! Two super-fiends in a ghastly plot against each other! The shadow of the black cat over all!

With David Manners, Jacqueline Wells, Lucille Lund, Henry Armetta, Egon Brecher. Produced by Carl Laemmle, Jr. Directed by Edgar G. Ulmer. Presented by Carl Laemmle. A UNIVERSAL PICTURE.

Ad No. 1—4 Col. Mat 40c, Cut $1.20

WILD! WEIRD! WICKED!

BLACK CAT

KARLOFF and BELA LUGOSI

in a story suggested by EDGAR ALLAN POE

With David Manners, Jacqueline Wells, Lucille Lund, Henry Armetta. Produced by Carl Laemmle, Jr. Directed by Edgar G. Ulmer. Presented by Carl Laemmle. A UNIVERSAL PICTURE

Ad No. 2—2 Col. Mat 20c, Cut 50c

Ad No. 3—1 Col. Mat 10c, Cut 25c

BLACK CAT

Ad No. 4—1 Col. Mat 10c, Cut 25c

The monster of "Frankenstein" and the monster of "Dracula" in a picture suggested by a story by EDGAR ALLAN POE

BLACK CAT

KARLOFF and BELA LUGOSI

in a screen epic of weird happenings that will make your hair curl with its chills as you thrill to its dramatic conflict and deep mystery.

With David Manners, Jacqueline Wells, Lucille Lund, Henry Armetta. Produced by Carl Laemmle, Jr. Directed by Edgar G. Ulmer. Presented by Carl Laemmle. A UNIVERSAL PICTURE

IT'S TREMONSTROUS!

Because the monster of "Frankenstein" is in it! Because the monster of "Dracula" is in it! Because the eerie imagination of EDGAR ALLAN POE is in it!

THE BLACK CAT

KARLOFF and BELA LUGOSI

in the most thrilling story of unheard-of wickedness the screen has ever known! . . . A girl in the clutches of a monster who would preserve her beauty forever! Her lover battling he knew not what! Two super-fiends in a ghastly plot against each other! The shadow of the black cat over all!

With David Manners, Jacqueline Wells, Lucille Lund, Henry Armetta, Egon Brecher. Produced by Carl Laemmle, Jr. Directed by Edgar G. Ulmer. Presented by Carl Laemmle. A UNIVERSAL PICTURE.

111

POSTERS

WILD!
WEIRD!
WONDERFUL!
SUPER-PAPER TO SELL IT!

THE THRILLIFIC 24 SHEET

6 SHEET →

3 SHEET A ←

TURN TO PAGES 9 AND 10 FOR ADDITIONAL POSTERS AND ACCESSORIES

PRINTED IN U.S.A.

The Black Cat: Universal's Symphony of Horrors
The Film's Music
by Randall D. Larson

Heinz Roemheld - Courtesy of Wm. H. Rosar

The early 1930s were seminal days for Universal's growing cycle of horror films. Emerging from the silent era during which they reigned with such influential macabre thrillers as *The Hunchback Of Notre Dame* and *The Phantom Of The Opera*, both starring Lon Chaney, Universal quickly transitioned into the sound era with the a series of innovative monster movies, many of them starring contract monster men Bela Lugosi and Boris Karloff. Films such as *Dracula, Frankenstein, The Mummy,* and *The Invisible Man* resulted in iconic monster creations that are still being reinvented today.

Other films did not generate franchise-worthy creatures, but were superbly created standalone films of early Gothic or modernesque horror, like *Murders in the Rue Morgue, The Old Dark House, The Raven,* and *The Black Cat.*

In addition to inventing the monster movie with these pictures, a similar evolution in the use of music in films was occurring in these same motion pictures. The studio's silent films had contained plenty of music – playing via live orchestras, solo piano or theater organs –

largely used to counter the complete absence of sound or to mask the noise of early film projectors. With the advent of the talking pictures, though, music tended to be phased out unless there was some kind of visible source showing where the music came from (a radio, or a restaurant band) appearing on the screen, in order not to confuse audiences, who might be distracted by wondering where the music was coming from in a particular scene. The use of musical underscoring as an enhancement to the film's drama was not yet recognized – Laemmle evidently felt that music in films was only a temporary trend, perhaps leftover from the silent era, and would not last. Thus *Dracula*, *Frankenstein*, and *Murders in the Rue Morgue* contained no music at all, except for mood-setting orchestrations that played over those films' titles. It was 1932's *The Mummy* that featured the tentative use of dramatic incidental music for the first time in a Universal monster movie.

When rival studio RKO released *King Kong* in 1933, with a stupendous and near wall-to-wall symphonic score by Max Steiner, the notion of music as a dramatic component of fantasy and horror movies was finally established, and Universal began to take notice. While 1933's *The Invisible Man* contained only a sparse eight minutes of original scoring,[1] the studio's next film, *The Black Cat*, contained nearly wall-to-wall musical featuring dramatic underscore. *The Black Cat*'s pervasive and influential use of music, at this early era in the use of films in cinema, is particularly ironic in view of Laemmle's adamant opposition to its use in this film. Fortunately cooler heads prevailed.

At the behest of the film's director, Edgar G. Ulmer, the film was scored with classical music, carefully inserted to reflect the refined taste of the film's villain, Hjalmar Poelzig (Boris Karloff) and support the film's various moods of mysterioso, tortured romance, suspense, and horror. "With the exception of *Fantasia*, *2001*, and *A Clockwork Orange*, no other sound film embraced the classics from head to tail," noted cinema historian Paul Mandell.[2]

"The score for *The Black Cat* is the longest and most substantial in [Universal's early] horror film series," wrote William H. Rosar in his seminal essay on early Universal monster movie music. "Of *The Black Cat*'s sixty-five minutes, fifty-five contain music. As had become common practice in the silent film era, Roemheld employed motifs for the main characters and appropriate mood pieces for situations."[3] Many of the score's pieces consist of piano music, which Roemheld arranged for full orchestra and then modified as necessary to fit the length of the scene or action it is accompanying. Rosar

adds that about half of the score is comprised of Roemheld's variations on classical pieces as well as original compositions of his own; "the remaining half being actual quotations from the works of classical composers."[4]

To make such a patchwork of musical excerpts enhance the film's visual drama, Roemheld selected classical pieces to be employed as leitmotifs associated with the main characters or used to augment events as they transpired in the story. Thus, *The Black Cat* not only received the largest amount of any Universal sound horror film up to that time, it was also the first to take full advantage of the idea of dramatic themes to interact with and reflect nuances of the film's characters. This technique would continue in the monster movies that followed, *The Raven*, *The Werewolf of London*, and *The Bride of Frankenstein* (all 1935) until it eventually became de rigueur for Hollywood film scoring.

Born in Milwaukee in 1901 of German parents, Heinz Roemheld had studied in Berlin to become a concert pianist. During the 1920s, he served as music director at Milwaukee's Alhambra Theater, conducting the pit orchestra for silent movies. The theater's owner was Carl Laemmle; when he heard Roemheld's musical accompaniment for a showing of Lon Chaney's *The Phantom of the Opera* in 1925 he was so impressed that he contracted Roemheld to work in a number of his other theaters as musical director. Laemmle, who was also the founder of Universal Pictures, brought Roemheld to Hollywood in 1929 as a staff composer, and then appointed him general musical director there the following year.

Roemheld thus held a significant role in the musical orientation of the studio's earliest horror films of the sound age that included serving as music director of the 1931 rerelease of 1923's *The Hunchback Of Notre Dame*, 1930's *The Cat Creeps* (a sound remake of the 1927 thriller *The Cat And The Canary*), and also handling the musical treatment of *Dracula* in 1931, including adapting its main title music (an abbreviated movement from Tchaikovsky's *Swan Lake* deftly arranged to fit the running time of *Dracula*'s main titles) and the classical pieces heard during at the concert hall scenes in London. By the end of 1931 Universal had decided to dissolve its music department, claiming it had sufficient recorded music and that any new compositions needed would be commissioned by contract; through this means Roemheld was hired back to compose the music for *The Invisible Man* and by the time *The Black Cat* crept onto the studio schedule in 1934 Roemheld was once again a regular Universal composer.

By 1934 Roemheld had had four years of experimenting with the use of music in sound films, in addition to his years of experience selecting and performing published music used to accompany silent films. "So when not composing new music, Roemheld had an almost uncanny knack for selecting appropriate existing music to score films when called upon to do that," said Rosar in a 2003 lecture at Stanford University.[5] The score was recorded with a 50-piece orchestra, a luxury compared to the norm in Hollywood at that time.[6]

Along with Ulmer's request, the presence of specific pieces of classical music accompanying the film dramatically were actually dictated in the screenplay by Peter Ruric (having no doubt been specified by Ulmer), although when it came to post-production Roemheld chose different pieces than those suggested in the script – with one exception: the ubiquitous *Toccata and Fugue in D. Minor* by Bach, heard when Poelzig plays the organ (a piece that has become virtually mandatory for any horror film when a dangerous character plays the organ; its use in *The Black Cat* is one of its earliest placements in film, preceded primarily by usage in Rouben Mamoulian's *Dr. Jekyll and Mr. Hyde* from 1931).

In addition to the classical music, Roemheld incorporated into the score a piece of his own music originally for string quartet, "Emeline," written for his wife, which was used when Joan recovers after being treated for her injuries by Werdegast. Along with Roemheld's original pieces based on classical themes used briefly or incorporated as transitions between the classical works, nearly all of the classical pieces heard in the score bear his own musical personality. "Roemheld's own style intrudes at almost every opportunity," Rosar emphasized in his lecture, "but in such a way that it doesn't detract from the quoted pieces."[7] Thus, one cannot replicate the musical soundtrack to *The Black Cat* simply by taking those familiar pieces from classical records and compiling them together; the music is colored through Roemheld's personal musical lens and remains distinctly his either as a paraphrase, adaptation, or orchestration.

To reflect the urbane aristocracy and refined tastes of Boris Karloff's devil-worshipping Poelzig whom Ulmer wanted to portray as an *arbiter elegantiarum* ("judge of fine taste"), Roemheld selected the first theme from Liszt's *Piano Sonata in B Minor* as his character's musical motif. It was a befitting piece of music in its diabolical sonority and progression, which suited the atmosphere and malevolency of the Satanist Poelzig. Written in 1853, the sonata is a complicated programmatic work rich in resonance and suggestion, which according to one commentary, has been said to convey at its core "inspirations ranging from Milton's *Paradise Lost* and the biblical tale of Adam and Eve to speculations that the Faust legend as well as the story of Genesis – of God and the devil,

creation and annihilation, sin and redemption – are at its core. Liszt himself never even hinted at such a possibility and there is no clear evidence to support such interpretations. However, it would be fair to assert that the composer's deep spirituality, strong Catholic values, and faith influenced his music in general and specifically the sonata's rich thematic material and strong emotional charge."[8]

Thus was this selection of music ideal to represent sonically the unsavory character of the Satanist Poelzig, while also befitting the Hungarian locale of the film story.

To underline Bela Lugosi's psychiatrist Dr. Werdegast, Roemheld selected another piece from Liszt, the opening of the symphonic poem *Tasso, Lamento e Trionfo* (Tasso, Lament and Triumph), written in 1849. The piece is based on the 16th century poet with emphasis on the man's inner conflicts, his unjust commitment to an insane asylum, and his eventual recovery. In *The Black Cat*, Werdegast is similarly troubled and in search of redemption; he visits Poelzig's home to accuse his host of war crimes and of spiriting away his wife during his incarceration as a prisoner of war. The excerpt from *Tasso* well represents his ongoing bereavement and vengeful intent as well as subtexts that his character shares with the titular poet. At one point Poelzig himself calls Werdegast an "avenging angel."

Traveling with Werdegast and his servant Thamal (Harry Cording) are a pair of young American honeymooners, Peter and Joan Alison (David Manners and Julie Bishop); all of them become imprisoned in Poelzig's monstrous Bauhaus-inspired home after Joan is injured in a vehicle accident while en route to a resort. Offering a much lighter and more innocent tone, a somewhat jazzed-up modification in contemporary style of Tchaikovsky's *Romeo and Juliet* love theme is used as the "Cat Love Theme" for the young lovers; a secondary motif associated with Peter alone is inspired by the slow movement of his *Symphony No. 6 in B-Minor (Pathetique)*. Finally, for Karen (Lucille Lund), Werdegast's daughter who Poelzig has married, and whose mother (also named Karen) he murdered and keeps encased in glass as a frozen memorial in his cellars, Roemheld assigned Brahms' "Sapphic Ode" ("Sapphische Ode"), the fourth song from his Lieder cycle *Five Songs for Low Voice with Piano Accompaniment*, written in 1884. The piece, originally transcribed for voice and piano, lends a haunting fragility to her mysterious character. Brahms's delicate romantic poem was based on poet Hans Schmidt's "Rhymed Sapphic Ode" which described a singer's walk through a rose garden at night, recalling the memory of a lost love; it well fits the younger Karen's mysterious appearances and behavior (despite its title, neither Schmidt's poem nor Brahms's *Ode* convey elements of female homosexuality, but gain their titles due to Schmidt adopting the lyrical form of the female Greek poet, Sappho [c. 600 B.C.] in his work.)

These four motifs form the thematic basis of *The Black Cat* score, while additional excerpts of Liszt, Schubert, Chopin, Bach, Beethoven, Schumann, and Tchaikovsky-derived music are used to augment the mood of various scenes. Roemheld's selection of music for these scenes clearly benefitted from his familiarity with the measures and moods of the classical canon achieved during his years as an accompanist for silent movies. They are both fitting and articulate, resonating with the environments as well as the dramatic subtexts suggested by the film. For example, the opening scene, a montage at a Hungarian train station, naturally prompted the use of Liszt's *Hungarian Rhapsody #3*. Later Roemheld will use the "Rakoczy March," from Liszt's *Hungarian Rhapsody #15* to similar effect when Poelzig's monolithic home first comes into view, reinforcing its unsavory military history (the massive home was built upon the foundations of a wartime fortress, Marmaros, from which the edifice has taken its name; this choice of music reflects the military past of Poelzig's home). This same march is adapted later for a humorous scene with visiting local gendarmes (a piece Roemheld entitled "Hungarian Burlesque") – again the music reinforces a cultural reference. During the chaotic storm when the bus carrying Werdegast and the honeymooners to Poelzig's castle crashes, Roemheld deftly inserts an excerpt known as the "storm" music from Liszt's symphonic poem *Les Preludes*. This piece is reprised later in the film during a more diabolical tempest, when the trees blow furiously beneath a cloudy sky when Poelzig communes with unseen demons as he prepares to sacrifice Joan in a satanic ritual (here, *Les Preludes* is climaxed by a chordal statement of the Liszt *Sonata* theme to reflect Poelzig's satanic authority). A particularly effective excerpt from Beethoven's *7th Symphony* – a hymn-like arrangement of the second movement (allegretto) – is heard during Poelzig's reflective monologue while escorting Werdegast through the chambers of Marmaros, lending a sardonic sense of nobility and self-assurance to Karloff's delivery. "The haunting allegretto... underscored the subjective camera's retreat from the basement and Karloff's disembodied monologue," wrote Mandell. "In its wailing melody is suggested resignation, futility, and the resurrection of dreary wartime memories."[9] The film's Main Title mixes the Liszt *Sonata*, and the Tchaikovsky-inspired Love Theme in a seamless construct. The *Sonata* begins the main title music in a severe agitato variant. Here, kicked into gear by Roemheld's

timpani and onrushing strings, the orchestral arrangement barely resembles the original piano piece in form. Instead, it reflects the kind of propulsive monster music that started off most of Universal's horror pictures of the era, yet manages to bear a touch of pathos remaining in the *Sonata's* elegant melodic line – four rising arpeggios from strings and brass, the fifth note echoing the fourth before dropping quickly off with a cluster of four descending notes, the surging tone and ferocious propulsion of timpani and winds kicking up an undercurrent of writhing menace. Roemheld then smoothly segues into the lyrical "Cat Love Theme" as the titles shows principal cast and supporting players before seguing into Roemheld's arrangement of Liszt's *Rhapsody* as the film opens on the bustling Budapest train depot. Throughout the score that follows, Roemheld will integrate the various themes and motifs like an expert basket weaver.

There are a couple of examples in *The Black Cat* where music begins as source music but then assumes the more interactive role of dramatic music. The first movement of Schubert's *Unfinished Symphony* begins as incidental music heard from a radio in Werdegast's guest room, until its progression matches Werdegast's fright at seeing a black cat (he has a phobic fear of them) and his killing of the creature in a rage. The shock passes and a lyrical sonority accompanies Joan as she enters the room, caught in a medication-induced trance; as Poelzig describes the phobia that led to Werdegast's killing of the cat, the music segues into a more ominous tonality. The scene "is a beautifully realized melding of music," wrote the authors of *Universal Horrors*. "It's timed with absolute precision, skillfully edited and rather daringly staged by Ulmer."[10] Noted Paul Mandell, "The whole sequence seems to glide along with a kind of lyrical ballet rhythm, and the footage was edited to correspond with the crescendos and diminuendos."[11]

As both Rosar and the film's cue sheet[12] suggests, the Schubert symphony was not Roemheld's arrangement, carefully timed to fit the sequence of events, but rather an existing recording arranged by Universal orchestrator William Schiller – Ulmer edited the sequence to the music.[13]

Schumann's *Piano Quintet in E-flat* is associated with the cellars where Poelzig hides the evidence of his Satanism and his necrophiliac obsession with the dead. Roemheld claimed that the Schumann *Quintet* was often used as a funeral march, which makes its association with Poelzig's cellars and the atmosphere of death quite appropriate. Schumann's *Quintet* is the second of two pieces in the Black Cat score that Roemheld did not orchestrate; it was arranged by Otto Langey[14] and had previously been used in the non-dialog version of 1930's *All Quiet on the Western Front* (when Lew Ayres tries to comfort a French soldier he has mortally wounded in combat).

While the main theme of the first movement of Tchaikovsky's *Pathetique Symphony* inspired Roemheld's theme for Peter, its second movement is modified into the menacing, metronomic music that accompanies Poelzig down into his cellars, where his collection of dead women are preserved behind glass. Roemheld paraphrased all the Tchaikovsky material rather than quoting it directly because it was not yet in the public domain and the music budget did now provide for licensing the music, so he opted to simply modify it into something new. Thus Roemheld composed new themes entitled "Cat Love Theme" and the theme "Dialogue" for Peter inspired by the Tchaikovsky symphony. The cue "Cat Threat" was likely based on Tchaikovsky's *Marche Slav* (Slavonic March), heard near the end of the film when Werdegast, mortally wounded by Alison, ignites the dynamite which brings Poelzig's house down.

Roemheld told Rosar that he had about a week to score *The Black Cat*, which may be impossibly short by today's standard, but with Roemheld's skill and experience it was close to normal. "In the silent days, working with a music librarian, Roemheld probably had less than a week to do just this kind of selection," albeit without also composing original music, Rosar noted in his Stanford lecture.[15]

The Black Cat: Music cues

By comparing the cue sheet to the film the following list identifies the classical pieces used in *The Black Cat* in film sequence:

• 1. Liszt: *Piano Sonata in B Minor* - Main Title music first half, as orchestrated by Roemheld (as throughout the score).
• 2. Tchaikovsky - *Romeo and Juliet* (Cat Love Theme) - Main Title music, second half; segues to:
• 3. Liszt: *Hungarian Rhapsody #3* - opening montage at the Budapest train depot.
4. James Huntley: *Jazz Karikaturen* - music in a contemporary jazz style as Peter and Joan are introduced in their train car. In spite of its German title (Jazz caricatures) the music is very distinct in comparison with the European music of the opening, and suggests the Americanness of the young couple. Music continues through until Werdegast arrives to share their car.
5. Liszt: *Tasso, Lamento e trionfo* - Werdegast gazes

out the train window; camera cuts to fireman shoveling coal and train wheels churning. Roemheld's cue, entitled "Hungarian Train" on the cue sheet, consists of a medley of Tasso, the theme of Liszt's *Hungarian Rhapsody No. 1*, and "Cat Love Theme," and concludes (orienting the music to Werdegast) with the "Tasso" theme as Werdegast runs his fingers through sleeping Joan's hair, remarking to Peter how she reminds him of his lost wife.
6. Liszt: *Les Preludes* "storm" music - bus crash in the storm; segues to:
7. Liszt: *Hungarian Rhapsody #15*, "Rakoczy March" - first view of Poelzig mansion; segues to:
8. Chopin: *Piano Prelude No. 2* - the trio's entrance into Poelzig's mansion, orchestrated by Roemheld.
9. Liszt: *Piano Sonata in B Minor* - introduced when Poelzig quickly sits up in bed, having been notified via intercom of Werdegast's arrival; segues to:
10. Tchaikovsky - *Romeo and Juliet* (Cat Love Theme) - Werdegast, the doctor, treats Joan's wound from the bus crash. Called "Cat Neutral" in Roemheld's version, this paraphrase is low-keyed and incidental; segues to:
11. Liszt: *Tasso, Lamento e trionfo* - Appears during Peter's close-up beside the injured Joan and play through the end of the scene until Poelzig appears.
12. Liszt: *Piano Sonata in B Minor* - Poelzig enters the room; closes with a paraphrase of "Tasso" when Werdegast and Poelzig confront each other menacingly. Sonata resumes as Poelzig escorts Werdegast out of the room.
13. Tchaikovsky - *Romeo and Juliet* (Cat Love Theme) - concludes the scene after Poelzig and Werdegast exit, as Peter gives his sleeping wife a gentle kiss.
14. Schubert: *Unfinished Symphony*, first movement - After an innocuous bit of small talk between Poelzig, Werdegast, and Alison, Werdegast's ailurophobia is set off by the arrival of a black cat, which he impulsively kills; Joan glides in, under the effect of Werdegast's medication; Poelzig explains the doctor's phobia of cats. The music, initially heard coming from a radio, assumes dramatic properties (what is called "source scoring" in film music) as it is arranged to match the scene's dramatic peaks; segues to:
15. Tchaikovsky - *Romeo and Juliet* (Cat Love Theme) - "Cat Love Theme," as Peter carries his wife to bed and tucks her in for the night before rejoining the other two men.
16. Liszt: *Tasso, Lamento e trionfo* - In the hallway, Werdegast explains how the drug he gave Joan caused her to act as she did, and he and Poelzig discuss the mythology of the black cat.
17. Tchaikovsky: *Pathetique Symphony*, first movement - Werdegast offers to switch rooms with Alison so he can be next to Joan's room. This motif is associated with Peter Alison.

18. Tchaikovsky – *Romeo and Juliet* (Cat Love Theme) – a brief interlude as Peter looks in on Joan briefly, before returning to the *Pathetique*, first movement.

19. Tchaikovsky: *Pathetique Symphony*, second movement – transformed into Roemheld's "Morgue" with its metronome beat as Poelzig wanders the cellars regarding his collection of glass-encased dead women; continues as he confronts Werdegast in his room, after mistakenly challenging Peter.

20. Liszt: *Sonata/Tasso* – In a Roemheld arrangement entitled "Fantasy on Two Liszt Themes," the *Sonata* is imposed over Poelzig's intruding into Werdegast's room, waking instead Alison, who has moved into Werdegast's room. The music quickly segues into *Tasso* as he realizes his error, and Werdegast enters through the door between the adjoining rooms. *Tasso* continues in Roemheld's cue, "Dialogue," as Poelzig and Werdegast have an awkward chat in the latter's room.

21. Schumann: *Piano Quintet in E-flat* – Poelzig takes Werdegast down into the cellars and shows her the preserved corpse of his wife, Karen.

22. Liszt: *Tasso, Lamento e trionfo* – heard in a brief reprise as Poelzig and Werdegast jointly mourn the dead Karen. Roemheld then inserts a brief shock moment of his own, entitled "Cat Scream," an agitated stinger as Werdegast pulls his gun on Poelzig, but is interrupted by the appearance of another black cat and he falls back.

23. Beethoven: *7th Symphony*, allegretto movement – Music begins after Werdegast's collapse and continues through Poelzig's monologue as he escorts Werdegast back up to the house.

24. Brahms: "Sapphic Ode" ("Sapphische Ode") – poignantly expressed by the strings as Poelzig returns to bed and speaks to the younger Karen (Werdegast's daughter and now Poelzig's wife).

25. Liszt: *Tasso, Lamento e trionfo* – As interpolated in a cue called "Introduction and Religioso," Roemheld's music here accompanies Werdegast as he dissuades his manservant Thamal from going to kill Poelzig. This is followed by a religious-sounding chiming motif for celesta, woodwinds, and strings, as the scene returns to Poelzig's bedroom as, beside the sleeping Karen, he peruses the *Rites of Lucifer* book he keeps on his bed stand. The tune seems modeled somewhat on a portion of Tchaikovsky's *Serenade for Strings* in its descending hymn-like cadence.

26. Roemheld: His composition "Emeline" is heard as the scene transitions to the following day with a shot of clouds passing overhead, and Joan waking, freed of the narcotic haze of her medication, as Werdegast kindly looks in on her.

27. Liszt: *Piano Sonata in B Minor* – a brief phrase of the descending melody, which is called "Karloff Theme" on the cue sheet, is sounded in double-octave strings as Poelzig abruptly enters the room and leers at Joan.

28. Tchaikovsky – *Romeo and Juliet* – The "Cat Love Theme" is reprised as Peter is sent for and embraces Joan, pleased to see her recovering; reprised two scenes later as they embrace again, alone and more passionately, in her room.

29. Liszt: *Hungarian Rhapsody #15* – a variation on "Rakoczy March" that Roemheld entitled "Hungarian Burlesque" heard during the awkwardly comical scene with a quartet of local gendarmes who come to investigate the bus accident.

30. Tchaikovsky: *Pathetique Symphony* [et al] – While Poelzig and Werdegast play an uneasy game of chess, Alison requests that he and Joan he allowed to leave. For this extended sequence, Roemheld wrote a medley incorporating a number of pieces into a consecutive series of cues he entitled "Introduction," "Dialogue," "Light Agitation," "Cat Foreboding," and "Cat Suspense." "Dialogue" is drawn from the jazzed-up string version of *Pathetique*'s opening movement (Peter's theme); the other cues are based on the agitato music of the symphony's first movement. A brief reference to Liszt's *Sonata* (aka "Karloff's Theme") is heard when Thamal assaults Peter as he tried to leave with Joan. Segue to:

31. Schumann: *Piano Quintet in E-flat* – After Thamal knocks Peter out, Joan faints and is carried by Thamal to her room and locked in by Poelzig.

32. Liszt: *Tasso, Lamento e trionfo* – Thamal takes the unconscious Alison and locks him in a secret dungeon room in the cellar.

33. Bach: *Toccata and Fugue in D-Minor* – Relaxing after his concealment of the Alisons, Poelzig playing the organ, unaware that Werdegast has absconded with the key to Joan's room. The organ music plays in the background as Werdegast unlocks Joan's room and tells her his plan, and of Poelzig's Satanism.

34. Liszt: *Tasso, Lamento e trionfo* – this cue resumes as Werdegast relocks Joan's room and goes to see Poelzig.

35. Roemheld – "Cat Crawl" – a brief gesture for violins imitating a cat "meow" emphasizing the black cat that startled Joan when it emerges from the next room through an open connecting door.

36. Brahms: "Sapphic Ode" ("Sapphische Ode") – Following the cat, the young Karen emerges into Joan's room; realizing who she is, Joan informs her that her father, Dr. Werdegast, is not in fact dead, but is "in this very house."

37. Liszt: *Piano Sonata in B Minor* – A severe presentation of harsh, descending chords bespeaks danger as Poelzig, hearing their conversation through the door, enters and confronts them. A wicked glare sends Karen away; Poelzig leaves Joan alone and pursues Karen, strangling his wife (off screen) to preserve his plans.

38. Liszt: "Storm" music from *Les Preludes* – Poelzig communicates with unseen Satanic forces in preparation

for the evening's sacrificial rite.

39. Bach: *Toccata, Adagio, and Fugue in C* - Poelzig leads his satanic congregation to the ceremony room. The organ is played by an unidentified cult member (a part performed, uncredited, by John Carradine, seen only from behind) as the ritual begins. Other cultists bring Joan, who is to be the diabolical sacrifice, as Poelzig intones in Latin.

40. Brahms: *Rhapsody in B Minor* (agitato from beginning, orchestrated by Roemheld) - Aided by Thamal, Werdegast acts - freeing Joan from the ceremonial altar when Poelzig is distracted by a cultist's scream. Meanwhile, Peter escapes from his dungeon

41. Liszt: *Sonata/Tasso* - An "Allegro Appassionato" by Roemheld continues from the Brahms piece as Thamal saves Werdegast from one of Poelzig's thugs but is shot in the process, and Joan informs Werdegast that his daughter is here, but Werdegast finds her dead. The twin Liszt pieces accompanies the final, violent confrontation between Poelzig and Werdegast, with elements of Poelzig's theme (*Sonata*) and Werdegast's Theme (*Tasso*). Thamal, dying from being shot, helps secure Poelzig to his own rack used for embalming his sacrificial victims, and achieves his gruesome vengeance by skinning him alive with a surgeon's scalpel.

42. Tchaikovsky: *Pathetique Symphony* - Under the title "Cat Interlude," Roemheld inserts a brief and plaintive transition of his own as Peter appears, locked behind a steel grated door, and calls to Joan. Aided by Werdegast, Joan fishes the door key from the dead servant's pocket. Mistaking Werdegast's intentions, Peter shoots him in the back. The Alisons escape from the mansion.

43. Liszt: *Tasso* - Werdegast, mortally wounded, stumbles back against the wall, wearily regarding Poelzig on the rack.

44. Tchaikovsky: *Marche Slav* - Roemheld's "Cat Threat," likely adapted from Tchaikovsky's "Slavonic March," plays when Werdegast finds the switch that will ignite the dynamite held beneath the mansion, and pulls it.

45. Tchaikovsky - *Romeo and Juliet*- The "Cat Love Theme" triumphantly concludes the score as the Alisons, flagging down a car that just happens to be driving by at that very moment, escape into the woods as the massive edifice of Marmaros detonates ono the hilltop and crumbles to rubble. The music continues as the scene segues to a final, cute moment with the couple on board the train taking them back to Budapest, and all is right with the world.

Postlude

The selection and arrangement of the classical motifs worked well in *The Black Cat*, heightening the drama in the manner of an original score, as film historian Calvin Beck has noted: "Though Hollywood musical scoring was still in its early stages and used haphazardly, it plays a vital part in elevating *Black Cat* to its classical level, at times endowing the principal players' movements with a lyrical opera-ballet rhythm underscored by variations from Brahms, Liszt, Tchaikovsky and others. Classical music in films has rarely been used with such grand effect and understanding..."[16]

"Roemheld's powerful score adds a good deal of passion, mood, and lyricism to *The Black Cat*, concluded Rosar, "both heightening and complementing the dramas synergistically, as a good score can. The amount and strength of the music in the film gives it a very musical quality."[17]

The effectiveness of Roemheld's music in *The Black Cat* evidently impressed Universal execs, as the monster films that followed all contained elaborately thematic film scores, Karl Hajos' music for *The Werewolf of London* (1935) heralding a concise but well integrated musical structure, and Franz Waxman's score for *The Bride of Frankenstein* (1935) setting the new standard for which the studios' musical trend would follow.

But that trend would largely be without Roemheld at the helm. Aside from creating an extensive score for *Dracula's Daughter* (1936) and having his music from earlier films, including *The Black Cat*, recycled by Universal throughout the ensuing years, Roemheld was largely absent from the Universal monster factory until the later 1950s. He began a lengthy association with Warner Bros. from 1934 through 1945, after which he freelanced for a variety of studios following World War II. Cues of his were occasionally reused in Universal factory approach scores to *The Mummy's Tomb* (1942), and he contributed new cues to *The Mole People* (1956), and *The Land Unknown* (1957); he then composed his last horror score for 1957's *The Monster That Challenged The World*, concluding his horror film pedigree by creating one of his finest scoring efforts, and one that, uncharacteristically for Universal horror films of the 1950s, was 100% original Roemheld. While these later horror efforts were notable, Roemheld's most important (and mostly unrecognized) significance in the fantastic cinema remains in his contributions to the moody horror films of Universal during the early pioneering days of both the horror film and its music. Of these, 1934's *The Black Cat* is likely the most significant and innovative.

Long-time film music journalist Randall D. Larson currently writes a film music column for buysoundtrax.com and is the author of more than two hundred soundtrack album commentaries and several books on film music, including *Musique Fantastique: 100 Years of Science Fiction, Fantasy & Horror Film Music* (www.musiquefantastique.com).

Thanks to David Schecter for fact-checking assistance. And a very special thanks to William H. Rosar for his peer review of this essay, and for his excellent and thoroughly-researched article, "Music for the Monsters," published in the *Quarterly Journal of the Library of Congress* (Fall 1983), which has been a significant reference source for me in my studies of the early Universal Studios film music. Quotes from Rosar's article are used with his permission. (Rosar's full article has been archived online at https://www.academia.edu/769153/Music for the Monsters Universal Pictures Horror Film Scores of the Thirties .)

(Endnotes)

1   See my essay, "'I've Just Heard The Invisible Man!' Music and Monsters in Universal's Early Horror Period,"in *The Invisible Man*, Universal Film Script Series, ed. Philip J. Riley, MagicImage Filmbook series #17, BearManor Media, 2013, p. 195.

2   Mandell, Paul, "Enigma of The Black Cat" [modified from an article in *American Cinematographer* magazine, Vol. 65, No. 9, Oct, 1994]
The Cinema of Adventure, Romance and Terror (Hollywood, CA: The ASC Press, 1989), p. 193.

3   Rosar, William H., "Music for the Monsters," *Quarterly Journal of the Library of Congress* (Fall 1983), p. 403.

4   Rosar, p. 404.

5   Rosar, William H., "The Black Cat: The Composer's Point of View," Lecture in series "Reviewing the Canon: Borrowed Music in Films", Stanford University Dept. of Music, May 3, 2003. Speaker's notes, revised Oct. 11, 2013, p.5. (Rosar interviewed Roemheld often about this score and others).

6   Rosar, Lecture, p. 7.See also Gregory Wm. Mank, paraphrase of *Hollywood Reporter* news item, April 13, 1934, p. 46 of this volume.

7   Rosar, Lecture, p.7.

8   Kirov, Milen, "Notes on Piano Sonata in B Minor, S. 178, Franz Liszt," Posted online at http://www.laphil.com/philpedia/music/piano-sonata-b-minor-s178-franz-liszt, undated. Accessed Aug. 21, 2014.

9   Mandell, p. 194.

10   Weaver, Tom, Michael Brunas, and John Brunas, *Universal Horrors*, Second Edition (Jefferson, NC: McFarland & Company, 2007), p 93.

11   Mandell, p. 194.

12   A legal document prepared by the studios that lists every bit of music used in a film by title, composer, and publisher.

13   Rosar, Lecture, p. 11.

14   Rosar, email to the author dated 8/24/14.

15   Rosar, Lecture, p. 6.

16   Calvin Thomas Beck, *Heroes of the Horrors* (New York: Macmillan Publishing Co., 1975) p. 128-129.

17   Rosar, "Music for the Monsters," p. 404.

About the Author

Gregory William Mank won acclaim in 1981 for his first book, *It's Alive! The Classic Cinema Saga of Frankenstein*. Subsequently he authored the published books: *The Hollywood Hissables; Karloff and Lugosi: The Story of a Haunting Collaboration; Hollywood Cauldron; Hollywood's Maddest Doctors; Women in Horror Films, 1930s; Women in Horror Films, 1940s; and Bela Lugosi and Boris Karloff: The Expanded Story of a Haunting Collaboration*, for which he won a Rondo Award for Best Book of 2009, as well as a Rondo for Writer of the Year. He has written the production histories for 12 of the previous MagicImage books, is co-author of Dwight Frye's *Last Laugh* (with James T. Coughlin and Dwight D. Frye) and *Hollywood's Hellfire Club* (with Charles Heard and Bill Nelson), and has written many magazine articles. He wrote and recorded the audio commentaries for the DVD releases of *Abbott and Costello Meet Frankenstein, Dr. Jekyll and Mr. Hyde, Cat People, The Curse of the Cat People, The Mask of Fu Manchu, Chandu the Magician, The Mayor of Hell, The Walking Dead, and Island of Lost Souls*. He has appeared on the TV shows *E! Mysteries and Scandals, Entertainment Tonight, and Rivals,* and on many documentaries on film history. A graduate of Johns Hopkins University and Mount Saint Mary's College, MD, he also has enjoyed a career in education and in theatre. His upcoming book is *The Very Witching Time of Night: Twists and Tangents in Classic Horror.* Greg lives with his wife Barbara in Delta, Pennsylvania. Visit his website, www.gregorymank.com.

Bud Abbott
Ralph Bellemy
Robert Bloch
Ray Bradbury
Ivan Butler
John Carradine
Ben & Ann Carre
Patric Leroux
Lon Chaney Jr.
Mae Clarke
James Cagney
Bramwell Fletcher
Robert Florey
A.Arnold Gillespie
Valerie Hobson
David S. Horseley
Henry Hull
Paul Ivano
Zita Johann
Elsa Lanchester
John Landis
Rouben Mamoulian
Lester Matthews
Patsy Ruth Miller
Jeff Morrow
Mary Philbin
Vincent Price
Ricou Browning
Ben Chapman
Jack Arnold
Joseph Stefano
Chris Costello

William Alland
Raymond F. Jones
Charles Van Enger
Joseph Gerserson
Alexander Golitzen
Walter Lanz
Gloria Stuart
Raymone Massey
Martin Scorsese
Curt Siodmak
Kenneth Strickfaden
Edward Van Sloan
Wallace Worsley Jr.
Peter Coe
Paul Malvern
Carla Laemmle
Carl Laemmle Jr.
Josephine Hutchison
Bela Lugosi Jr.
Sara Karloff
Virgil Miller
Walter Rankin
Hans Salter
Elana Verdugo
David Manners
Stanley Bergerman
Paul Kohner
Franklyn Coen
Gloria Holden
Otto Kruger
Lou Wasserman
Ron Chaney